AF174039

MAGNUS HIRSCHFELD

Magnus Hirschfeld, 1930

Magnus Hirschfeld
The Origins of the Gay Liberation Movement

RALF DOSE

translated by Edward H. Willis

MONTHLY REVIEW PRESS

New York

Copyright © 2014 by Ralf Dose
All Rights Reserved

Originally published as *Magnus Hirschfeld: Deutscher – Jude – Weltbürger*
by Verlag HENTRICH & HENTRICH, Berlin, Germany
© 2005 Verlag HENTRICH & HENTRICH
English translation published by Monthly Review Press, 2014

Monthly Review Press
146 West 29th Street, Suite 6W
New York, New York 10001
www.monthlyreview.org

5 4 3 2 1

Contents

Introduction to the U. S. Edition

TODAY, THE NAME Magnus Hirschfeld is once again familiar to many people, at least to those who take an interest in the history of the homosexual rights movement. Perhaps they've seen Rosa von Praunheim's film, "The Einstein of Sex." I've written this book in response to the renewed interest in a long-forgotten personality. It is intended to provide a brief survey of Hirschfeld's life and of the central topics in his work. The German edition of this biography appeared in 2005 as part of the series "Jüdische Miniaturen" ["Jewish Miniatures"] published by Hentrich & Hentrich. That text has been translated and revised to reflect the most current state of research.

Magnus Hirschfeld was descended from a German family of Jewish origin; he was a Social Democrat, a co-founder of the field of sexology as an independent discipline, and a pioneer in the struggle for homosexual rights. He was a "militant scientist who sought to combine science with humanity and justice."[1]

Hirschfeld's doctrine of "sexual intermediacy" was an attempt to provide a place for homosexual men and women in nature, and thereby a place in society. This was an unheard-of concept, but it was derived from exacting observations. It made fluid the border between male and female in an age that still made enormous and unbending distinctions between the sexes and their respective "natural" attributes. Today there is renewed discussion about the full implications of this concept.

"Through science to justice" was Hirschfeld's motto. Permeated as he was by the ethos of the Enlightenment, science became a means to his end purpose of achieving social justice. During his lifetime, he was the subject of controversy, both because of his claims and because of his demands. He was controversial because his science was not completely objective and because both his research interest and his social cause were in effect society's sexual outsiders. His name is inseparably linked with the struggle against Paragraph 175 of the German penal code, which made homosexual conduct among men a punishable offense. In this, too, Hirschfeld was far ahead of his time. Paragraph 175 was not struck from the German penal code until sixty years after his death.

When the Germans ostracized Hirschfeld as a Jew and took his country from him, he was forced to define himself anew. "German—Jew—or world citizen?" he wrote in 1933, at the beginning of his exile. "World citizen" or "all three" was his decision.[2]

After the Second World War, Magnus Hirschfeld and his works were nearly completely forgotten. Partly to blame in Germany and Europe were the Nazis, from whom Hirschfeld had been able to save only himself. His institute in Berlin and his scientific legacy were destroyed, save for a few scant remains.

Outside Europe, Hirschfeld had attracted some attention with his 1930–32 world tour. But despite his significance for science and for a nascent international homosexual rights movement none of his major works appeared in English during his lifetime: neither *Naturgesetze der Liebe* (The

Natural Laws of Love) nor *Die Homosexualität des Mannes und des Weibes* (Homosexuality of Men and Women), neither *Die Transvestiten* (Transvestites) nor the three-volume *Sexualpathologie* (Sexual Pathology), let alone the five volumes of *Geschlechtskunde* (Sexology). Hirschfeld remained unknown in the English-speaking world. The fact that during his world tour he was presented as "the Einstein of sex" in the American press, and that several smaller works were reprinted in English in various rather remote locations, made little difference. To give readers an indication of the breadth of Hirschfeld's work, I have supplied a bibliography at the end of this book.

Hirschfeld only lived long enough to see the English and American editions of his travelogue, *Die Weltreise eines Sexualforschers* (*Men and Women: The World Journey of a Sexologist*). An unauthorized and abridged translation of *Sexualpathologie* appeared as *Sexual Pathology* in 1932. Harry Benjamin sent Hirschfeld a scathing report: "The one English translation I know of the first volume of your *Sexualpathologie* is here being sold at $5 by irregular booksellers. It is a most atrocious translation, utterly impossible; and a man by the name of 'Jerome Gibbs' has signed responsibility for it. It was published by the Julian Press, Newark, 1932."[3]

In 1936, there appeared in England under Hirschfeld's name an apocryphal screed, reprinted in the United States in 1944 and later translated back into German, called *Sexual Anomalies and Perversions*. It was actually a compilation by Arthur Koestler. Albert Ellis was highly critical of this book: "Although *Sexual Anomalies* gives, in clear and brief form, a fairly comprehensive outline of the human sexual deviations, and while it is an adequate summary of the works of a renowned pioneer and liberal, it adds little to our insight into the etiology of the anomalies which it describes."[4]

Another of Hirschfeld's books (*Racism*, London 1938) did appear in English, but only in English. Its readership seems to have been small, just like the series of articles on which it was based, which appeared in Prague in a German-language newspaper for exiles from the Third Reich. Only today is it becoming clear that by using the word "racism" Hirschfeld created a concept that only much later developed its full meaning.

After the Second World War, discussion within the field of sexology was dominated on the one hand by psychoanalytic theories and on the other by the empirical methodologies of Alfred Kinsey.[5] It was not until the late 1960s that an alignment of interests between sex research, now sociologically oriented, and the gay liberation movement was renewed. In this context, slowly and haltingly, Hirschfeld's works were rediscovered. Haltingly because both his foundation in biology and genetics and the grounding of his sex research within medicine made him appear questionable, or even suspect, in the eyes of a new generation of activists. The controversy continues today: authors such as Simon LeVay (2011), who claims to have observed structural differences between the brains of heterosexuals and homosexuals, or Dean Hamer, who postulates a genetic contingency for homosexuality, can easily be located in the research tradition of Magnus Hirschfeld. These and similar lines of argument for "naturalness" are still (or again) used by parts of the liberation movement to fend off homophobic attacks.[6]

Nevertheless, Hirschfeld's activism and his significance within the early homosexual liberation movement were so obvious and inescapable that they could no longer be ignored. Most recently, especially in the context of the development of "queer theory," Hirschfeld's comprehensive theory of "sexual intermediacy" has been appreciated with an entirely new kind of interest.[7]

Hirschfeld's combination of science and activism was held against him by both medical and political colleagues during his lifetime. "Science" is supposed to be objective. That was the position of psychiatrist Albert Moll.[8] Within the gay rights movement, the position has also been taken that there must be no reliance upon "beggarly" medical theories,[9] but instead a determined struggle for human rights, solely in the political realm.

After the Second World War, Hirschfeld was completely forgotten in Germany, except by those few remaining who had been his colleagues or fellow activists. During Hirschfeld's lifetime, German had been a world language, in which scientists outside Germany had at least a reading ability. After the war, only language specialists were in a position to read his works. It was just such specialists, our friends in the United States, who gave back to us this suppressed history of the first German homosexual rights movement and spurred our curiosity about our own predecessors. James D. Steakley's painstakingly researched bibliography, "The Writings of Magnus Hirschfeld," which appeared in Toronto in 1985, started a search for Hirschfeld's publications that is still not complete today. Among the items Steakley marked "not autopsied," many still have not surfaced. Others, like the many interviews Hirschfeld gave during the 1930–32 world tour, may not yet have been identified for research purposes.

Not until a second gay rights movement developed, and began to take an interest in its own history, were a pair of Hirschfeld's main works translated into English by Michael Lombardi-Nash, with the publishing support of Vern Bullough: *The Homosexuality of Men and Women* and *Transvestites*. The latter book especially makes clear that Hirschfeld's work was of interest not only for homosexuals but encompasses a much broader spectrum of "sexual intermediate stages," which today are described using abbreviations like LGBTQ (Lesbian, Gay, Bisexual, Transgendger, Queer). Here I must refer to a book, which is not by Hirschfeld, though he sponsored the original publication and he supplied an epilogue. The author used the pseudonym N. O. Body, and the book is called *Aus eines Mannes Mädchenjahre* (Memoirs of a Man's Maiden Years). It was written by Karl M. Baer, who was the director of the Berlin lodge of B'nai B'rith until his emigration to Palestine in 1938.[10] It is a first-person account by the first individual to undergo a female-to-male sex-change operation. An English translation by Deborah Simon was published by the University of Pennsylvania Press in 2009.

As part of the rediscovery of Hirschfeld, English-language biographies were also written. First was Charlotte Wolff's 1986 contribution, though it has been out of print for quite a while. Like Hirschfeld, she was a refugee from Germany. As a young woman doctor in Berlin, she had been his contemporary, but she only became interested in his works in her later years. Quite recently, Elena Mancini, in her book, *Magnus Hirschfeld and the Quest for Sexual Freedom: A History of the First International Sexual Freedom Movement*, has attempted to do justice to Hirschfeld's contribution to gay liberation.[11]

Today the name Magnus Hirschfeld, sex researcher, is known again in Germany, and this author is proud to have contributed to this change through his work with the Magnus Hirschfeld Society in Berlin.

Introduction to the German Edition

"PROFESSOR MAGNUS HIRSCHFELD—even his physical appearance is certainly the most repulsive of all Jewish monsters." Thus did the Nazi author Hans Diebow vilify the sex researcher in his sorry 1937 effort *The Eternal Jew*.[12] In the same year a copy of Hirschfeld's bust was displayed in Nuremberg at the so-called Museum of the Revolution with a sign reading: 'The lovely Magnus Hirschfeld—the greatest rooting swine* of the 20th century.'

Who—and what—was this man who made the Nazis wish to parade him in public as a prime example of the hated Jew?

Dr. Magnus Hirschfeld, M.D. and Medical Councilor, born in Kolberg, Pomerania (today Kołobrzeg, Poland) in 1868, was known during his lifetime as one of the most prominent sex researchers in Germany and far beyond. He

---

*Although the primary meaning of the term "rooting swine" (in German, *Rübenschwein*) is a pig rooting in a vegetable garden without license, readers in the 1930s would have recognized a reference to the language of the trenches in the First World War, when it referred to soldiers who never raised their heads high enough above the trench to risk being exposed to enemy fire. —*Trans.*

helped create this field of study and was chairman of the Scientific-Humanitarian Committee—the first organization that advocated rights for homosexuals—and, as of 1919, director of the Institute for Sexual Science in Berlin, which he founded. In 1933 the Nazis put a brutal end to his work; Hirschfeld was on a world tour at the time and never returned to Germany. He died in 1935 in exile in Nice.

After 1945, Magnus Hirschfeld was forgotten, not completely, to be sure, but the few surviving members of his circle were not in a position to build upon the successes of the 1920s and carry on his work. His closest associates were either dead or did not return from exile, and the few survivors were not able to perpetuate his tradition after the Second World War as they were anchored neither in academic life nor medicine. The homosexual rights movement, far reduced in importance by comparison with the 1920s, had virtually no means of public expression in Germany during the 1950s and '60s. In 1962 the propaganda of the Nazis was embedded so firmly in the minds of the people and in the legal code of the Federal Republic that Hans-Joachim Schoeps (1909–1980) was forced to observe: "For homosexuals the Third Reich has not yet come to an end."[13]

Magnus Hirschfeld was not able to found a "school." As a non-academic institution, his Institute for Sexual Science had a limited capacity to further professional careers. Besides, Hirschfeld was a man of "distinct partialities and dislikes," as Ludwig Levy-Lenz (1885–1972) described his friend at the institute,[14] and he was not able to train a crown prince or successor who would and could continue his work. During the 1920s there were several persons in whom Hirschfeld placed hope in this regard. They declined, however, and either went into other specialties or were themselves such strong personalities that Hirschfeld was not able to "form them in my image"[15] as much as he would have liked. In the end, there remained two young friends and followers: Karl Giese, who took his own life in Brünn (now Brno, Czech Republic) in 1938, and Li Shiu Tong of Hong Kong. Neither man was able to fulfill his wishes.

Hirschfeld's concept of homosexual emancipation, as he expressed it in his Latin motto Per scientiam ad justitiam—"through science to justice"—is certainly still current today, though under different scientific auspices and without direct reference to Hirschfeld as predecessor. Hans Giese (1920–1970) and his German Society for Sexology attempted in the 1950s, as Hirschfeld had earlier, to use scientific findings to make an impact on the provisions of the German penal code regarding homosexuality. In the 1970s and '80s similar attempts were made using sociological arguments.

Hirschfeld and his work were only rediscovered after the formation of a new homosexual rights movement that, starting in the early 1980s, went about finding its historical roots. As was soon discovered, Hirschfeld's is a complicated legacy. The debate about it has just begun.

His Life

FAMILY

MAGNUS HIRSCHFELD WAS born on May 14, 1868, in Kolberg on the Pomeranian coast of the Baltic Sea, the son of the physician Hermann Hirschfeld and his wife, Friederike.

His father, Hermann Hirschfeld, M.D., came from Neustettin (today Szczecinek, Poland); his mother's maiden name was Mann, and she came from Bernstein an der Warthe (Pełczyce, Poland). Both families were related: Hermann's father and Friederike's grandmother were siblings. Friederike Mann was married young. Hermann Hirschfeld visited the sixteen-year-old in Berlin, where she was being educated at a girls' boarding school, and then requested that a mutual friend of both families convey his proposal of marriage. They were married two years later (1855).

Hermann Hirschfeld completed his medical studies, including a dissertation, with Rudolf Virchow (1821–1902). The appended curriculum vitae in Latin includes at the very beginning this proud avowal: "Judaeus sum"—"I am a Jew." Hermann Hirschfeld belonged to the generation of those who studied at the Berlin University (renamed Friedrich-Wilhelm University in 1829 and Humboldt University in 1949) during the uneasy period prior to 1848. After his education he performed his required military service in Schleswig-Holstein during the Prussian war against Denmark and in 1850 opened a medical practice in Greifenberg (Gryfice, Poland), and moved to Kolberg two years later. As a Prussian garrison town, Kolberg had for many years (until 1812) denied any right of immigration to Jews. But beginning in 1822, a Jewish community in Kolberg can be documented. It was still very small when the Hirschfelds moved there, and Hermann Hirschfeld, just as he became established, was chosen as a member of the Jewish community's Deputy Assembly, an organ of self-government in which nearly all adult Jewish males were assigned functions. He was the only "man of learning" among the merchants and was reelected many times, into his old age. In 1871 he became president of the Jewish community. At this point in time, he was a well-known man in the city. Standing in the tradition of his teacher, Rudolf Virchow, he had already rendered outstanding services, helping to create the sewer system and provide running water to Kolbergermünde, a district lying outside the old town walls, improvements that were necessary for the development of Kolberg into a seaside resort. For a time, Hermann Hirschfeld also owned his own sea-bathing and saltwater spa facility, called the North Bath (Nordbad), but his enterprise was not destined for financial success. For medical services rendered to the French soldiers imprisoned during the 1870–71 war—about 5,000 prisoners were held at Kolberg, which had a population of just 20,000—Hermann Hirschfeld earned a Prussian commemorative medal. Finally, comparatively late in life, he was appointed Medical Councilor. The residents of Kolberg honored their beloved physician one year after his death (1885) by placing a monument on the Promenade (today u. Spacerova), after taking up a collection for it around the city. The Committee for the Erection of a Monument united the Jewish community, the city councilors, the local press, the Sailing Club, those in trades and businesses, and even the Lutheran chaplain from the local army base. Less than fifty years later, the citizens of Kolberg could no longer tolerate a monument to a Jew in their city—it was destroyed immediately when the Nazis came to power in 1933.

Little is known about Friederike Hirschfeld, née Mann (July 6, 1836–1905), who survived her husband by about twenty years. Friederike had eight siblings, among them the attorney and notary Dr. Julius Mann (1853–1931). Up until his death, legal councilor Julius Mann was president of the Jewish community in Stettin (Szczecin). The marriage between Hermann and Friederike produced ten (perhaps eleven) children: before Magnus, her sons Emanuel (also Immanuel) and Eduard, of whom the first became a physician and the second a pharmacist. Emanuel emigrated to the United States, where he worked in a Catholic hospital in Milwaukee and later operated a clinic in Winnetka, Illinois, north of Chicago. He died in Davos, Switzerland, in 1925. After Eduard's pharmacy business failed, he followed his brother to America, but died from injuries sustained in an accident shortly after opening a medical practice in Chicago. His son Hermann then lived with his uncle Emanuel, then during his apprenticeship (at the machine engineering firm Orenstein & Koppel) with his aunt Franziska Mann in Berlin. Later, with the help of his uncle Magnus, he had a business as a stamp dealer in Berlin. He survived the Nazi period under difficult conditions in a so-called mixed marriage and returned to the United States in 1953, where he was known as Harry S. Field. Eduard's widow, Elise, née Weil, lived in Hamburg with her stepdaughter, Röschen

(Rosa Kantorowitz, Eduard's first wife, had died shortly after their marriage). Both were deported and murdered.

Magnus Hirschfeld's sisters were Recha, Agnes, Franziska, and Jenny. Other sisters—Blancka, Margaretha, one unnamed sister, and Olga, of whom there is no official record—died as young children. During 1886 and 1887, Richard Kantorowicz from Posen lived with the Hirschfeld family as a foster brother. He earned his baccalaureate with Magnus in 1887 at the Kolberg Dom-Gymnasium (Cathedral School), later became a researcher in Africa, and for a time was the German Resident Minister in Rwanda.* He was baptized Protestant in 1893 and took the surname Kandt, as did all the male members of his family.

Hirchsfeld's oldest sister, Recha, married Martin Tobias, who came from a Jewish family long established in Mecklenburg. The couple moved to Teterow and had three children. In 1890 Martin Tobias took over a saltwater spa facility in Kolberg from the widow of Moritz Behrend—a colleague and competitor of his father-in-law. The affiliated guest house was still operated by Recha Tobias after 1900. Later, the Tobias family also lived in Berlin. In the 1920s, the widowed Recha moved into an apartment in her brother's Institute for Sexual Science and rented rooms to visitors. Her son Georg was an eye doctor in Biesdorf near Berlin. He survived the war in a mixed marriage. Recha was deported to Theresienstadt at a very advanced age in 1942 and died shortly thereafter. Her daughter Marga also became a victim of the Shoah; her son Gustav and his wife died in Berlin during the air raids.

---

*The German *Resident*, "Resident Minister," or Resident-General, was a diplomatic post with duties of colonial governance. Rwanda became a German colony in 1884. Control passed to Belgium during World War I. Rwanda became independent in 1962.—*Trans.*

Agnes remained unmarried and operated Dr. Hirschfeld's family guest house in the home of her parents in Kolberg until her death in 1922. Jenny married Julius Hauck from Steinau and lived in Berlin and Kolberg; their marriage was unhappy and they lived separately. After the death of her sister Agnes, Jenny inherited the guest house in Kolberg and named it in Agnes's memory as "Villa Agnes." Of their children, a daughter, Eva, died in 1924 of scarlet fever; their son Rudi married Gerda Betty Marcuse in 1930. Both of them escaped the Nazis in 1938 with their newly born daughter, Ruth Gabriele, fleeing to England and then to Australia. Jenny and Julius Hauck are buried in the Jewish cemetery in Weißensee, Berlin.

Franziska also was not happy in her marriage. Her husband, Moritz Mann, one of her mother's brothers, was a hotelier, first in Stettin, then later in a central Berlin location at the Passagen-Hotel, part of a famous new indoor shopping mall at the corner of Behrensstraße and Friedrichstraße. Franziska Mann achieved a reputation as a writer. Loneliness, the most prevalent theme in much of her writing, was not unknown to her in her own life. She had three sons, two of whom died shortly after she did. Both of them, like their parents, are buried in the Jewish cemetery in Weißensee. The third escaped the Nazis, fleeing to England.

In Kolberg, Magnus and his brothers and sisters had happy childhoods. Reflections of it may be found in the works of Franziska Mann, but also in memorial articles in the *Kolberger Zeitung für Pommern* (Kolberg News for Pomerania), which Magnus and Franziska jointly dedicated to their father on the hundredth anniversary of his birth in 1927. Even though Hermann Hirschfeld's work as a physician was widely appreciated, as was his weekly column in the *Kolberger Zeitung*, it is rather amazing that neither Magnus nor Franziska mentions his last and most important office.

The fact that their father was for many years a member of the Jewish community's Deputy Assembly and finally its chairman is not found in their memoirs. His office cannot have remained without influence on his family life. They give no report of how Jewish traditions were kept in their parents' home. Only once, in a completely different context, is it mentioned that the family gathered on Friday evenings at the home of their grandmother.[16] Whether they observed the Sabbath on these occasions we do not know.

As a university student, Magnus designated himself a "dissident" after the first few semesters. We can conjecture that something similar applies to Franziska. Only in the guestbook that Magnus Hirschfeld maintained while in exile do we find a reference to the religious education he enjoyed: in it he preserved a memento honoring Dr. Salomon Goldschmidt (1837–1927), for many years the Kolberg rabbi.

UNIVERSITY STUDIES

WHEN HIS FATHER DIED, Magnus was seventeen years old and still attending the Kolberg Cathedral School. Hermann Hirschfeld had not been able to lay much by to provide for his family, so relatives had to pay for his education. Presumably, his uncle Julius Mann in Stettin was one of his supporters. From 1887 to 1894, Magnus studied in Breslau (now Wrocław, Poland), Strasbourg (at that time part of Germany), Munich, Würzburg, and Berlin. He first enrolled to study modern languages, then he decided for practical reasons on medicine: "I left my first love on my own accord," he wrote, looking back in 1928, "but I was not unfaithful, for when I later changed to the study of the natural sciences and medicine, it was more for external reasons. Inwardly, all my life long I've felt more closely and essentially connected to journalists, men of letters, writers, poets and artists than I have to doctors, professors and very privy superior Medical Councilors.* While I regard the latter as my colleagues and mentors, I perceive the former as my comrades in the freedom fight for the Beautiful, the Good and the True."[17]

By studying in Strasbourg for two semesters (1888–89), Magnus Hirschfeld was continuing a family tradition: his brothers Emanuel and Eduard had also spent time there, studying and completing their military service. In 1890 Emanuel worked as a medical doctor in the Alsatian mining town St. Kreuz im Lebertal (St. Croix-aux-Mines, France). Hirschfeld remembered a teacher from his student days in Strasbourg who had a formative impact on him: the pathologist Friedrich Daniel von Recklinghausen (1833–1910), who urged his students: "Observe, gentlemen, observe!" Hirschfeld saw in him a genuine "disciple of Virchow and that tendency which during the first decades of the last century focused on doing away with the speculations of Naturphilosophie and replacing theoretical considerations with exact data." He later laid claim himself to doing precisely this in his own area of specialization: "Uranianism† is

---

*With "*Wirkliche geheime Obermedizinalräte*," that is, "very privy superior Medical Councilors," Hirschfeld gently mocks the titles awarded by the Imperial government. The title Rat (Councilor) was awarded to persons with significant achievements in their chosen fields. Thus, there were Medical Councilors, Legal Councilors, Commercial Councilors, etc., even after the Empire was defeated in the First World War and a republic established. Naturphilosophie refers to a tradition in German philosophy extending back to Idealism.—*Trans.*

† "Uranianism," derived from the language of Plato's *Symposium*, refers to male homosexuality. This terminology was also used in nineteenth-century Britain.—*Trans.*

not a phenomenon that can be comprehended by the light of a study lamp, but only by studying the object itself."[18]

During 1889–90 Hirschfeld studied in Munich. From there, he visited the priest Sebastian Kneipp* (1821–1897) in Wörishofen, Bavaria. Naturopathy was not a subject in university instruction. Interested students had to seek out advanced training on their own.

Following his preliminary medical examinations in February 1890, he did military service for half a year in Würzburg, whereupon he completed his clinical semesters, three of them in Heidelberg, one in Berlin. On December 8, 1891, he passed his oral examination with Emil du Bois-Reymond (1818–1896), at that time Dean of the Medical Faculty of the Friedrich-Wilhelm University. On February 13, 1892, he was awarded an M.D., after the successful defense of his dissertation. The psychiatrist and neurologist Emanuel Mendel (1839–1907) provided him with his dissertational topic: "On Diseases of the Nervous System Attendant upon Influenza." His examination committee included, in addition to du Bois-Reymond, the surgeon Heinrich Adolf von Bardeleben (1819–1895), the gynecologist Adolf Gusserow (1836–1906), and Professors Gerhardt and Virchow. Hirschfeld took his state medical examination in Würzburg in 1893.

In the summer of the same year, he took his first long trip abroad, to Chicago to see the World Exposition and to visit his American relatives. His brother Emanuel was living north of

---

*Sebastian Kneipp (1821–1897) was a Bavarian priest and among the founders of naturopathy or natural medicine. He is best known for his hydrotherapies. He advocated whole meal bread. While working as confessor at the monastery at Wörishofen, he began offering water therapies and other therapies to local people and was soon providing therapy for princes as well.—*Trans.*

Chicago at that time, and the family of his father's brother, who had emigrated even earlier, was living in nearby Milwaukee, Wisconsin. He paid for his trip by writing newspaper reports (since lost). On his way back from the United States, he visited North Africa and Italy, before settling in Magdeburg-Neustadt and opening a naturopathic practice there in 1894.

FIRST PRACTICE IN MAGDEBURG: ACTIVISM FOR NATUROPATHY

WE DON'T KNOW EXACTLY why Hirschfeld settled in Magdeburg, but we do know that solar and fresh-air spas were affiliated with his medical practice and he provided hydrotherapies. Hirschfeld had learned the value of seawater, saltwater, and mud treatments from his father. At that time, Hirschfeld was one of only a few academically trained medical doctors who advocated and applied naturopathic procedures. Naturopathy was the domain of medical laymen, and medical doctors who advocated for it were putting themselves in conflict with their own profession. In Hirschfeld's case, controversy was not long in coming. The orthodox medical practitioners resident in Magdeburg accused Hirschfeld of malpractice in the treatment of blood poisoning in a patient from whom he was said to have withheld "invigorating alcohol." The patient died. The proceedings brought by the medical profession against Hirschfeld did end positively for him, and he titled his report *Ein Sieg der Alkoholgegner* (A Victory for Abstinence from Alcohol). But he was not able to remain in Magdeburg for long after this incident.

In 1896, Hirschfeld moved to Charlottenburg, which at that time was an affluent independent city outside the gates of Berlin. His first practice was in back of the City Hall (today Alt-Lietzow), but quite soon he moved to larger and more imposing premises in what was then Berliner Straße 121 (now Otto-Suhr-Allee 98, a new building). Diagonally opposite this address, the new Charlottenburg City Hall was built in 1899. Naturopathy remained one of the central subjects of his work. In Magdeburg, Hirschfeld had become active as a lecturer and writer for naturopathic journals. From 1896 to 1900, in addition to his practice, he edited *Hausdoctor* (Family Doctor), a "weekly journal for natural ways of health and living," in which he not only imparted medical advice for the layperson, but also shared inspiring articles and sometimes his own poetry. In 1897, he acted as examiner for the training course of the Association of Practicing Advocates of Naturopathy. In 1898–99, he taught a nine-month course of instruction in naturopathic anatomy and physiology.

Hirschfeld spoke out on many aspects of the *Lebensreform*, or Life Reform movement,* which at the end of the nineteenth and beginning of the twentieth century was taking a stand in Germany against the negative consequences of industrialization. Again and again, he spoke out in opposition to alcohol, but also in favor of the settlement movement, which, as part of the Life Reform movement, aimed to provide healthier living arrangements for workers. He signed the appeals of opponents of inoculation—at the time the first experiments with live vaccines against tuberculosis were taking place—and advocated healthy nutrition, in addition to light, air, and sun as the best preventative against the diseases of civilization. Hirschfeld was probably not a vegetarian, although he argued that proletarians should eat more healthy brown bread rather than fight over the bit of meat in the stewpot. In the 1920s, he participated in the nudist movement

---

*The settlement movement, part of the Life Reform movement, focused on creating modest suburban housing developments for urban workers. —*Trans.*

surrounding Adolf Koch. Tradition also has it that he was rather lax in following the strict sartorial customs of his day: he is said never to have worn a hat.

HIRSCHFELD'S PRIVATE LIFE

LUDWIG LEVY-LENZ (1889-1966) wrote about Hirschfeld's lifestyle and work habits in his memoirs:

> He began work at five in the morning seated in front of a big French window from which he had a wonderful view over the Tiergarten. Wherever he lived, he liked to have a wide prospect stretching away into the distance; it stimulated his mind....
>
> M. H. sought his recreation in music; the house in which he lived once belonged to the great violinist Joachim and it was that musician's spirit which presided over the concerts, over the trios and the quartets which, once a month, brought a crowd of eminent guests to the house....
>
> M. H. himself lived simply, his only luxury being a good table; but even in this he was limited by his diabetes, which denied him the enjoyment of his favourite dishes. He was not a very obedient patient, and unless he was watched, he would eat one piece of cake after another. Otherwise, he lived quietly amongst his books and in social intercourse with his intellectual equals—the life of a truly wise man.[19]

Hirschfeld never discussed personal matters. Any diaries he may have kept have been lost; and the series of auto-biographical articles, *Von Einst bis Jetzt* (From Then until Now),[20] written on the occasion of the twenty-fifth anniversary of the Scientific-Humanitarian Committee, though certainly a "history of a movement," leaves out any and all personal information. He considered himself a "public" figure, but knew how to keep his private life out of the public eye without actually concealing it. Thus we do not know whether he had a life partner or any long-lasting friendships or relationships before his fiftieth year—that is, before his friendship with Karl Giese (1898–1938). Would finding lost diaries provide information about this?

His sister Franziska mentions in her 1918 birthday letter that "you live all alone in your lovely house." It was at this time, certainly no later, but possibly as early as 1914, probably while making the educational film *Different from the Others,* that Magnus Hirschfeld met Karl Giese, a young working-class man. Karl moved in with Hirschfeld at the institute in 1919, where he looked after the collections and archives. Ellen Bækgaard (1895–ca. 1982) describes him in her memoirs as "the woman of the house." Accordingly, he is said to have enjoyed needlework and decorating the home. He also took care of Hirschfeld's wardrobe, since Hirschfeld was rather negligent in that area.

Despite their living in such close proximity to each other and frequently appearing in public together, it appears that "outsiders" could easily overlook the real nature of their relationship. Only after many years would Paul Krische (1878–1956), a long-standing colleague in the World League for Sexual Reform, and his wife, Maria (1880–1945), come to realize that not only Giese but their close friend Hirschfeld was homosexual, and that the two were a couple.

Others knew more. "You may well know that for me in Magnus Hirschfeld, not only my boss has died," Karl Giese wrote to Max Hodann (1894–1946) in England in the autumn of 1935 from exile in Brünn (Brno).[21]

In the last years of Hirschfeld's life there was a second friend, Li Shiu Tong (1907–1993) of China, and the two young men had to share Hirschfeld's affections. Max Hodann's second wife, at that time not yet divorced from him, met all three in Paris and then passed on this emigré gossip in a letter from Copenhagen (April 2, 1934) to Fritz (1874–1945) and Paulette Brupbacher (1880–1967) in Zurich: "Auntie Magnesia has been making his usual delightful mischief in Paris. He now lives with both flames (Tao and Karlchen). And best of all: both of them are sooo jealous of the old geezer. Surely that must be true love?!"[22]

Hirschfeld never explicitly "outed" himself. Such a public confession would have contradicted both his self-image and his role as a natural scientist, which was to investigate the world's phenomena without prejudice.

FINANCES

NOT MUCH IS KNOWN about Hirschfeld's financial situation. He had no inheritance from his father. His own medical practice and immense publishing activity apparently provided him enough income to make possible a solidly middle-class, if not upper-class, way of life, and occasionally gave rise to suspicions among his political opponents and others who envied him. For instance, one anti-Semitic hack job contained malignant rumors that Hirschfeld received disproportionately high fees from the Max Spohr publishing company for editing the *Jahrbuch für sexuelle Zwischenstufen* (Yearbook for Sexual Intermediacy), to the disadvantage of the Scientific-Humanitarian Committee; or even that he used knowledge gained from his practice to blackmail homosexual patients. If any portion of this had been true, his opponents would have done him in immediately. Doubtless, Hirschfeld was a prepossessing personality. Well-heeled patients paid considerable sums for consultation or treatment. Those without means were also treated. They could work off their debt, either doing clerical work in the offices of the SHC or, in the 1920s, in the household of the Institute for Sexual Science.

Investing his entire fortune—according to tax records for 1918 just under 400,000 marks, with a taxable income of 27,500 to 28,500 annually—in the purchase of a building for the institute proved to be a wise decision on Hirschfeld's part. At least the endowment's real estate could be preserved. The remaining endowment capital (according to various sources, between 30,000 and 100,000 marks) fell victim to inflation. The interest income designated for the defrayal of expenses for such a large house was no longer available. Hirschfeld noted in 1929 that he received no income from operating the institute, but earned his own living with publications, lectures, official reports, etc., yet he was not impoverished. At the end of the 1920s, his cousin, Leo Meyer, arranged for a financial stake in the Amsterdam department store Bijenkorf, which Hirschfeld regarded as a "nest egg" for the institute, and for himself.

Increasingly, Hirschfeld entered into contracts with the pharmaceutical industry, financially advantageous both for him and for the institute. The obligations arising from these contracts were a strain on Hirschfeld's medical ethics, and sometimes must have breached them. His contract with Vauka, the manufacturer of the so-called contraceptive Patentex, provided endorsements for the product that were not commensurate with verifiable medical findings, namely that Patentex was a reliable prophylaxis against an unwanted pregnancy. Hirschfeld and his colleague Richard Linsert (1899–1933) had already verified in earlier writings that this contraceptive jelly was only recommended for use together with a condom.

In the final years before 1933, Hirschfeld, the institute, and the institute's physician of many years, Bernhard Schapiro (1888–1966), received a more considerable income from marketing a remedy for impotence. "Testifortan" was an organ compound said to include in its ingredients (among them freeze-dried and pulverized anterior pituitary glands and testicle tissue from bulls) effective and standardized quantities of the male sex hormone (testosterone was yet to be fully discovered). Despite favorable reaction in the medical professional press, the medication was not initially a financial success for its manufacturer (Promonta in Hamburg) or its licensors. It only became successful when Hirschfeld and Schapiro entered into a contract with Max Baginski (1891–1964), an energetic Berlin entrepreneur who marketed Testifortan, with a minor change to the formula, to the layman under the brand name Titus-Perlen (Titus Pearls, perhaps named after the powerful Roman emperor Titus) both nationally and internationally. Hirschfeld apparently invested part of the royalties in the institute's ambitious journal *Aufklärung* (Enlightenment, that is, Sex Education). Later, it was doubtless these monies, in addition to the local lecture fees, that made possible a largely carefree world lecture tour (1930–32). After 1933, Nazi institutions, or with final authority the commercial department of the Berlin Police Presidium, received the royalty payments, and since then never returned Hirschfeld's share.

At the end of 1932, it became evident that the institute's long-standing administrative director, Friedrich Hauptstein (d. 1948), was unable to explain a discrepancy of nearly 90,000 marks between the income and the expenses of the institute and for some time had failed to submit the necessary annual financial statements to the foundation supervisory board (the foundation's file has been lost). Hirschfeld, who appeared to perform his supervisory duties laxly, did not want to believe that Hauptstein was lining his own pockets, but nonetheless withdrew his confidence in him as well as his power of attorney for the institute, which until then had been recorded in Hirschfeld's last will and testament. Hirschfeld estimated his assets, confiscated by the Nazis when the institute was closed in 1933, at 132,000 marks.

There are no records of how Hirschfeld financed his existence while in exile. His attempt to have the royalties for "Titus Pearls" paid directly to him by a pharmacist under contract to distribute the drug in Switzerland probably failed due to the foreign exchange regulations then valid in Germany. In the surviving records of the Zurich pharmacist, Dr. Hebeisen, there are no indications of any such direct payments. Hirschfeld was repeatedly forced to take out loans from his Chinese friend Li Shiu Tong, who came from a wealthy family. In France, Hirschfeld had some income from publishing contracts and journal publications. For instance, he was paid for a long series of articles in the illustrated *Voilà* in 1933, and for the translation rights to his writings by the publisher Gallimard. His means still allowed frequent travel. Early in 1935, he rented and furnished a large apartment in Nice as his home in retirement.

JUDAISM, ZIONISM, AND ANTI-SEMITISM

HIRSCHFELD'S CONSCIOUS REJECTION of his family's Jewish religious tradition can be dated to the first semesters of his university studies. In 1887, in Breslau, he still registered with the denomination "Jewish." Later, the same column always had the entry "diss." for "dissident," as a sign, he had left his parents' religious community but had not converted to one of the Christian denominations. Influenced by his scientific studies, especially his intense interest in the works of the biologist Ernst Haeckel (1834–1919) of Jena who made the teachings of Darwin popular in Germany. Through him Hirschfeld came into contact with monism, a type of scientific substitute for religion.

Hirschfeld kept few records regarding his contact with Jewish life or Jewish institutions in Berlin. As a "dissident," he was not a member of the community, nor did he observe religious customs. Like many Jews of his generation, he celebrated the Christmas holiday. The dates of his entries in "Testament: Notebook II" refer to Christian holidays.

The exact purpose or reason for his 1899 contribution to the Jewish convalescent home founded by Mr. and Mrs. Sachs in Lehnitz bei Oranienburg has not been explained. The home figured so strongly in local history that after 1945 the street leading to the home was named after Hirschfeld. Later the building housed a facility for mentally handicapped children, and in 1988 the building, by an initiative of the director at the time, was named the "Magnus Hirschfeld Home."

Hirschfeld's literary interests brought him into contact with Zionist thought. Near the end of his world tour, in Tel Aviv in 1931, Hirschfeld again met the actress Hanna Rovina (1889–1980). He had seen her in 1926 at the Nollendorf Theater in Habima Theater's Hebrew-language production of An-ski's *Dybbuk* (in an adaptation by Bialik).

As a student on his first trip to Paris, he had met Max Nordau (1849–1923), "in whose home in Paris . . . I spent a lot of time. At that time the differences of opinion were raging heatedly regarding the validity of the Zionist movement, which some saw as the only solution to the Jewish question, while others termed it 'succumbing to anti-Semitism' and feared an intensification of the extremes," he wrote retrospectively in 1935.[23]

These encounters did not result in Hirschfeld becoming a Zionist. At the very least, however, he did participate in a Zionist conference in 1917 (after the Balfour Declaration on November 2). He remembers a cheering crowd in the festively decorated Berlin Civic Center, when "the attorney [Alfred] Klee, well known to me from many court cases, a man of excellent intellectual acuity and utmost humanity, began his speech with the words: 'Jews! We have a country!'"[24]

He rejected the revival of the Hebrew language. He viewed it as promoting isolation, which would hinder commingling with one's neighbors. As elsewhere in his writings, Hirschfeld distanced himself from the kind of differentiation connected with the ideal of purity, which he felt was dangerous: "Experience has shown that linguistic isolation noticeably increases every nationalistic and chauvinistic instinct."[25] When the question "where to go" in exile arose, he was personally impeded from settling in Palestine by the language barrier, even though he had learned English to some extent on his world tour. The Holy Land, scene of the events in the Bible—he mentions the Hebrew Bible and the New Testament on conspicuously equal terms—was part of his heritage, both as an educated middle-class person and from the standpoint of cultural history. As a Life Reform activist, Hirschfeld had more in common with the young people on the beach in Tel Aviv:

> What a contrast . . . between the sobbing Chassidic youths along the Wailing Wall of Jerusalem and the fresh boys and girls on the beach of Tel Aviv, with the "beautiful spark of joy" flashing from their eyes! The attractive vitality and refreshing simplicity of these young people who proudly call themselves "chaluzim," that is, "pioneers," were one of the things in Palestine that made a deep impression on me. In their simple dress (hatless, bare-necked and with bare legs), in the ingenuousness of their manner, apparently strongly influenced by the modern movement of "Wandervögel" and the Boy Scouts, they seem so full of the joy, strength, and affirmation of life that they appear to have overcome all the repressions and unconscious feelings of erotic inferiority frequently found at this age.[26]

His own isolation, or at least distance, from his Jewish heritage naturally did not prevent Hirschfeld's enemies from defaming him as a Jew. Early on, there were anti-Semitic attacks. They became quite loud for the first time during the Eulenburg Affair (1905-08). The caricatures of the period always show Hirschfeld with a hooked "Jewish" nose. Emil Witte's inflammatory pamphlet, *Drei Siegfriedsrufe* (Three Calls of Siegfried),[27] of 1914 is an extreme example for this time period. But its vilifications found their way into the *Semi-Kürschner*,[28] an anti-Semitic reference work that dedicated many columns of its 1929 second edition to Hirschfeld. From there, these defamations could make their way directly into Nazi propaganda.

During the 1920s, the attacks continued and became violent. After a lecture in Munich, Hirschfeld was beaten up and left for dead. He had to see his own obituary in print. At that time, the Bavarian "humorist" Ludwig Thoma (1867-1921) repeatedly agitated against Hirschfeld in the *Miesbacher Anzeiger* (Miesbach Gazette), for the last time on August 2, 1921:

> The Apostle of Sodomy, the spinach specialist Hirschfeld, has called for a swine convention in Berlin this September. . . . This old Galician bastard has been pushing for public acceptance of sodomy as though it were for the public good. . . . This wretch has even tried to distribute his swinish propaganda in Munich, but a few sudden and well-placed blows have now shown that old bastard swine that he must grunt only in his stall in Berlin. That damned swine won't show up here again, because he can intuit that the next time his skull might be crushed.[29]

But it wasn't just right-wing cranks or nationalistic groups that defamed Hirschfeld as a Jew. In the 1920s, shrill anti-Semitic tones were also coming from his own camp, the organized homosexual-rights movement. For instance, distancing himself only halfheartedly, Adolf Brand (1874–1945) provided space in *Die Tante* (Auntie's), a "taunt and battle issue" of his journal *Der Eigene* (The Self-Owner) for Karl-Günter Heimsoth (1899–1934), who aimed vicious attacks at Hirschfeld under the heading "Love between Friends or Homosexuality."[30] Heimsoth later became infamous as a close friend of SA* Commander Ernst Röhm. In the same issue, Brand printed a caricature of Hirschfeld that might just as well have appeared in *Der Stürmer* (The Storm Trooper), a Nazi newspaper.

During the Nazi period of 1933 to 1945 the daily press continued to use Hirschfeld as a bogeyman, even long after he had died. Many propaganda pieces, even including materials from institutions like the German Museum of Hygiene, cited Hirschfeld as a prime example of the "Jewish type."[31]

It was the Nazis who forced Hirschfeld to acknowledge his own heritage. Initially he did so only defensively. Hans Blüher (1888–1955) made a note on something Hirschfeld supposedly said to him: "I must protest now being called a Jew and on these grounds being ostracized and persecuted by these Nazi swine. I am a German, a German citizen, just as good as any Hindenburg or Ludendorff, like Bismarck or our old Kaiser! An honest German, born in Germany to German parents! And so it was with me, as with just about any newborn child all over Europe: they are forced into religious straitjackets, are baptized or circumcised and meant to be reared in the faith of their parents. Because my parents

---

*SA refers to the *Sturmabteilung*, or Assault Division, the paramilitary wing of the Nazi Party. Ernst Röhm, who was comparatively open about his homosexuality, was murdered in a political putsch in 1934, largely because he presented a political threat to Adolf Hitler.—*Trans.*

adhered to the Mosaic faith, I have been marked with the Mosaic stigma!"[32]

Of course, the choice of words is more like Blüher than Hirschfeld, but what they express must certainly have been Hirschfeld's own position. Shortly afterward, he wrote in his own records: "The day of the Jewish Boycott—April 1, 1933—shall live on, but not alone in the history of Jewry! Recently, the humiliation and degradation of Jews has been making greater and greater strides from day to day, like that of the Blacks in America. As a freedom-loving person of Jewish descent, it appears to me that living in Germany, if one is not absolutely forced to, has become a moral impossibility. I have resigned myself to the idea that I shall never see Germany, my homeland, again, though it causes me great emotional suffering."[33]

In the end, he was not able to resolve this issue that had been forced upon him: "The question: Where do you belong—what are you really? tortures me. If I frame the question as: 'Are you a German—a Jew—or a world citizen?' then my answer is always 'world citizen' or 'all three.' "[34]

Independent of Hirschfeld's personal sense of belonging to a religious community and of his refusal to practice religion, some theorists, making reference to the positions espoused by Hermann Cohen, have located Hirschfeld's sexological positions in a philosophical tradition informed by Jewish values. It might be proved that "Hirschfeld's concept of history as the site of the realization of freedom is profoundly influenced by an ethos of justice derived from the messianic-prophetic tradition." His deconstruction of the bipolar sexes "occurred within the framework of a messianic-inspired concept of the history of liberation, but which overcame the theological worldview from which it arose."[35]

SOCIAL DEMOCRACY

BY HIRSCHFELD'S OWN ACCOUNT, he met August Bebel (1840–1913) during his university studies and found his way to social democracy through him. Because of this acquaintanceship Bebel introduced the petition of the Scientific-Humanitarian Committee into parliament in 1898, which most Social Democrats did not support.

Hirschfeld probably did not participate in party politics aside from this. The Imperial German Political Police did not even include Hirschfeld in their lists of doctors suspected of Social Democratic activities. However, Hirschfeld did appear as a campaign speaker for the party shortly after the end of the First World War. Around that time, he was also commissioned by Julius Moses (1868–1942), the Social Democrats' health policy expert, to create a draft of the responsibilities of a proposed Health Ministry. That text, published in 1919 as *Verstaatlichung des Gesundheitsewesens* (Nationalizing the Health Care System), shows the dilemma Hirschfeld faced: the nationalization of the health care system desired by the party's left wing would not be advantageous to him as a practicing doctor. As a successful medical entrepreneur, he rejected organizing doctors in polyclinics.

At the beginning of the 1920s, many older labor leaders from the SPD and USPD (Social Democratic and Independent Social Democratic parties) who were the same age as Hirschfeld and had attained government and parliamentary positions were visitors at the Institute for Sexual Science. In this way, Hirschfeld attempted to obtain political backing for his agenda of sexual reform. And in 1922, Hirschfeld's ally Kurt Hiller publicly advised the SPD to field Hirschfeld as a candidate for parliament, though the party did not follow his suggestion.

Like many of his coworkers at the institute, Hirschfeld was an active member of the Verein sozialistischer Ärzte (Association of Socialist Physicians), which for many years organized left-leaning doctors in a cross-party alliance. He had speaking engagements with them, and his institute was groundbreaking for his colleagues.

LITERARY INTERESTS

EVEN AFTER HIRSCHFELD had given up pursuing a degree in modern languages and transferred to medicine, he cultivated his literary interests and contacts. While a student in Munich, Hirschfeld earned extra income reading aloud for Henrik Ibsen (1828–1906) and was friends with Donald Wedekind (1871–1908), the brother of Frank Wedekind (1864–1918). After settling in Berlin, he and his sister Franziska socialized with the group surrounding the Hart brothers. As novelist and dramatist Hermann Kesten later scoffed:

> At the turn of the century the two Naturalist brothers Julius and Heinrich Hart founded "The New Community" together with Gustav Landauer and Felix Holländer, an "Order for True Living," which had a communal apartment in Uhlandstraße [Uhland Street] where Gustav Landauer, the radical Shakespeare commentator, and Erich Mühsam, the anarchist, prepared family meals, where Martin Buber and Magnus Hirschfeld gave alternate lectures on religious and sexual topics, and Peter Hille read aloud his poems.[36]

After the turn of the century, Hirschfeld paid regular visits, again often accompanied by his sister, to the writers' colony in Wilhelmshagen. He and Wilhelm Bölsche (1861–1939), who lived there, worked together for the Free University, the adult education facility Bölsche had founded.

Hirschfeld was also friends for many years with Else Lasker-Schüler (1869–1945), who not only dedicated a poem to him, but also frequently spent her summers in the guesthouse operated by Hirschfeld's sister Agnes, and later Jenny, in Kolberg. Among a younger generation of writers, Klaus Mann especially sought out Hirschfeld's acquaintanceship and friendship. Bruno Vogel (1898–1987), made famous by his 1928 novel *Alf,* was for a time an employee of the Scientific-Humanitarian Committee.

Hirschfeld's writing style was influenced more by his literary models than by scientific writing. He put special value on "being understood by everyone."[37] Many of his printed texts were developed from lectures. Hirschfeld also printed some of his attempts at poetry, although he was aware of the works' dubious quality. In the volumes of *Hausdoctor* (Family Doctor), which he edited, he sometimes included celebratory poems. He also printed a "Report in Verse" of his journey to Italy—in the footsteps of Johann Joachim Winckelmann, August von Platen, and Karl-Heinrich Ulrichs—titled *Drei deutsche Gräber im fernen Land* (Three German Graves in a Distant Land) in the 1909 volume of the *Jahrbuch für sexuelle Zwischenstufen* (Yearbook for Sexual Intermediacy).

MOVEMENT AND SCIENCE—THE ORGANIZER

The Scientific-Humanitarian Committee

IT WAS NOT ENOUGH for Hirschfeld to offer medical help to the sick and suffering on an individual basis. His father before him had sought political influence beyond his medical practice by advancing the development of his hometown into a seacoast resort with spa facilities and writing a weekly column in the *Kolberger Zeitung für Pommern* (Kolberg News for Pomerania). Hirschfeld fils did exactly the same, initially in the service of the naturopathy movement. But the topic he would devote his life to was edging into the foreground.

It was in Magdeburg that the event occurred that Hirschfeld later described as the origin of his medical and scientific engagement with homosexuality. A patient, a young military officer, committed suicide by shooting himself on the night before his own wedding, much anticipated by his parents. In his suicide letter to his doctor, he disclosed the reasons for his suicide and challenged Hirschfeld (who was then not yet thirty years old) to educate the hostile people surrounding him concerning the fate and fortune of homosexuals. At least that is how Hirschfeld tells this tale in his first brochure of the subject, *Sappho und Sokrates, oder wie erklärt sich die Liebe der Frauen und Männer zu Personen des eigenen Geschlechts* (Sappho and Socrates, or What Explains the Love of Men and Women for Persons of Their Own Sex). On the advice of the publisher, the brochure appeared under a pseudonym, Th. Ramien, which was subsequently never used again.

Six months later, in 1897, in his Charlottenburg apartment, Hirschfeld, together with a few other like-minded persons, including his Leipzig publisher Max Spohr (1850–1905), the railroad official Eduard Oberg (1858–1917) of Hanover, and the writer Franz Josef von Bülow (1861–1915), founded the Scientific-Humanitarian Committee (SHC), which he chaired until 1929. This committee marked the first successful creation of an organization that advocated homosexual rights. Earlier attempts, such as that of Karl-Heinrich Ulrichs (1825–1895) in the 1860s, had failed or had only limited effect.

The committee's main activity was petitioning for the repeal of Paragraph 175 of the German penal code, which dated from 1871. It criminalized male homosexual conduct.

From 1897 until the 1920s, petitions were repeatedly presented to parliament and failed each time. This petition is the founding document of the homosexual rights movement in Germany.[38] The list of signers, which grew continuously, reads like a *Who's Who* of German society. Hirschfeld and his early allies focused their efforts on doctors, lawyers, artists, teachers, and professors, and they met with much agreement. But they also faced fierce opposition.

With a peak membership of about 700, the committee, in addition to the petition campaign, developed a sex education program that was in great demand. It consisted mainly of lectures and a brochure, produced cheaply in large print runs, titled *Was soll das Volk vom Dritten Geschlecht wissen?* (What Must Our Nation Know about the Third Sex?).[39] Homosexuals requested it be sent to their relatives as informational material. It was distributed at events, or more widely by "intentionally forgetting" it in a vehicle of the public transportation system. Thus at the turn of the twentieth century, homosexuality became a fourth taboo topic, alongside venereal disease, prostitution, and contraception/birth control, that was demanding more and more public attention.

The members of the committee appealed directly to members of the professions and to the educated public, but in completely traditional ways. They published essays in professional journals or books, including medical publications. This was meant to fulfill Hirschfeld's supreme maxim: "Per scientiam ad justiatiam"—"through science to justice." At first he tried to determine which portion of the population was homosexual among various groups, such as metalworkers and students at technical universities. Sending out the questionnaire promptly earned him a libel action on behalf of students active in conservative and church groups. He also attempted to prove that homosexuality is a natural variant of human sexuality and thereby establish it as such. To this end, he applied what was then the most current and advanced medical knowledge and line of argument. Initially, he appealed to findings of genetic research to make plausible the naturalness and immutability of a homosexual person. Later, he put findings from hormone research (endocrinology) in the foreground. Because of particular hormone glands that functioned in a certain way and not in another, a person became homosexual or heterosexual, or perhaps something else entirely. The strategic goal of the arguments was always to prove "naturalness," which for Hirschfeld meant also the logical conclusion that penal sanctions were absurd.

Benedict Friedlaender (1866–1908), one of the intellectual members of the committee, described strategic differences that existed among the group: "We believe . . . that we don't really need a theory considered absolutely valid. . . Regarding our most basic issue, which is Paragraph 175, we can combat it using purely legal and moral arguments." He felt Hirschfeld's doctrine of sexual intermediacy turns homosexuals into "psychological freaks of nature," "pitiable half-women," and "poor female souls, languishing in male bodies." He considered it a "beggarly theory," which might inspire tolerance and sympathy but could not win respect or equality before the law.[40]

When the scandalous affairs involving the industrialist Friedrich Alfred Krupp (1854–1902), who committed suicide on Capri, or the imperial advisor Philip Count Eulenburg* (1847–1921) and his friends came to the public's attention, the committee tried to use these to their

---

*Philip Friedrich Alexander, Prince of Eulenburg and Hertefeld (1847–1921), after an obligatory military career was a politician and diplomat in Germany, and a composer and writer as well. His family was old Prussian nobility and had been serving the Hohenzollerns, now the Imperial

advantage. Some members, anticipating what would later be known as "outing," urged making public the names of high-ranking homosexual persons. They thought this alone would bring down the section in the penal code regarding

---

family, for generations. He became a doctor of law and received the Iron Cross during the Franco-Prussian War (1870–1871), which established the German Empire under Prussian rule. His diplomatic career, where he represented Prussia to other German principalities and kingdoms within the Empire, culminated in 1893 with his appointment to Vienna, capital of the neighboring Austro-Hungarian Empire, where he stayed until 1902. He was a close friend of Kaiser Wilhelm II (1859–1941). He was married to a Swedish aristocrat in 1875 and the couple had eight children. He also allegedly had homosexual contact with other members of the Kaiser's inner circle, including Count Kuno von Moltke (1847–1923), the military commander of Berlin, who was forced to resign in 1907 when this information was published in a Social Democrat aligned–publication called *Die Zukunft* (The Future) by Max Harden. The existence of the homosexual contingent in the Kaiser's inner circle was known, but Harden waited, gathering evidence, and began threatening Eulenburg with exposure in 1902. After waves of purges against soldiers and officers and accompanying waves of suicides in the military, including in elite corps, the scandal broke with this exposure, which launched a whole series of trials. Male homosexual activity was outlawed explicitly after German unification in 1871. Section 175 of the German penal code is known as Paragraph 175 and is based on earlier laws that had applied in smaller areas. Adolf Brand, homophile publisher of *Der Eigene* (One's Self) was sued for slander by Bernhard, Prince von Bülow, the Kaiser's Chancellor, who admitted he had heard stories about Eulenburg. Eulenburg denied these under oath and was then charged with perjury, but his trials were delayed due to ill health. Hirschfeld gave evidence in the proceedings between Harden and von Moltke and was forced to rescind his testimony at a later trial. Hirschfeld's professional reputation suffered because of his retraction and Harden regretted having caused the scandal because Kaiser Wilhelm II was even more aggressive and warlike without his accustomed favorites around him.—*Trans.*

homosexuality. Hirschfeld always rejected this "path over corpses" and thus exposed himself to the charge that he did not advocate the cause of homosexuals as articulately as he might. He did make a grave strategic error in one of the trials connected with the Eulenburg scandal, by attesting to "unconscious" homosexuality on the part of Berlin military commander Kuno von Moltke (1847–1923), without ever examining him personally. Hirschfeld was forced to revise his "expert opinion" during a second trial.

Hirschfeld's reputation never fully recovered from the consequences of that disaster. The committee, up till then a respectable and growing association, lost most of its membership and supporters. Hirschfeld's unwise and unmedical behavior also encouraged the open enmity of Albert Moll (1862–1939), who until then had been the undisputed medical expert on homosexuality and who felt slighted by Hirschfeld's prominent public appearances. Though Hirschfeld thought he was acting in the interests of the greater good, he created some reasonable doubts concerning his seriousness as a doctor and scientist.

Another conflict arose within the ranks of the committee and among its supporters. The public image of a homosexual man was defined by associations with terms such as "delicate," "effeminate," even "wearing women's clothing." Many homosexuals, however, including many committee members, did not accept the "nelly queen" or "auntie" as a prototype or positive role model. These homosexuals considered themselves "real men" and distanced themselves from "effeminate types." Instead, they advocated love between friends, to which nothing low or sexual adhered, and a pedagogical Eros that they understood as classically Greek.

Hirschfeld held such ideas in gentle derision, which he expressed in his discussion of a brochure by Erich Mühsam: "Friendship, however, which as Mühsam describes it, escalates into erotic love, is certainly not friendship, but love, precisely because it escalates into erotic love."[41]

It was this conflict that led Hirschfeld in the years that followed to differentiate transvestites—he coined the term—on a theoretical basis from other homosexuals, who had previously made up an undifferentiated group, and to establish a separate category for them.

After the disaster of the Eulenburg scandal, Hirschfeld went on a trip abroad (Holland, England, Turkey) and delved into substantial scientific research and publication projects. The Scientific-Humanitarian Committee was forced to redefine its purpose. Documenting the real lives of homosexuals in *Aus der Erpresserpraxis* (Blackmail and Its Victims) and fostering solidarity through social events became more important. But the struggle to reform the penal code remained the committee's most urgent task. When a proposed reform of the penal code that would also have criminalized homosexual acts between women became public in 1911, the committee began cooperating intensively with the radical wing of the German women's movement. Hirschfeld had previously had contact with Helene Stöcker (1869–1943), the leader of the Bund für Mutterschutz und Sexualreform (League for the Protection of Mothers and Sexual Reform). Now this contact was intensified and eventually deepened into a lifelong friendship.

During the First World War, the committee had to restrict sending care packages to their members at the front lines. Hirschfeld worked as a doctor in a Red Cross military hospital in Ruhleben, near Berlin. He was often asked to give his expert opinion regarding the fitness for combat duty of homosexuals, or when men were apprehended wearing women's clothing, assumed to be spies and slated for execution. At the beginning of the war, Hirschfeld published two nationalistic brochures based on lectures, *Warum hassen uns die Völker?*

(Why Do the Nations Hate Us?) and *Kriegspsychologisches* (On the Psychology of War). But when confronted with the horrors of war and under the influence of Helene Stöcker and Kurt Hiller, he soon became a member of the pacifist Bund neues Vaterland (League for a New Fatherland).

After the war was over and a republic had been established, the Scientific-Humanitarian Committee found that it had new competitors. In addition to the previously existing elitist Gemeinschaft der Eigenen (Community of Self-Owners) surrounding Adolf Brand, "friendship leagues" now sprouted up all over Germany, and were soon joined together in the League for Human Rights, which by the end of the Weimar Republic could claim 50,000 members. Members were mainly those who subscribed to journals published by Friedrich Radszuweit (1876–1932), who was also the league's chairman. The League for Human Rights was able to draw on a host of local groups. The Committee remained concentrated in Berlin, despite smaller groups that existed intermittently in Leipzig, Munich, Frankfurt, and Hamburg. Hirschfeld's leadership role in the homosexual rights movement was thus no longer as undisputed as it had been before the war.

The committee was gradually integrated into the new Institute for Sexual Science as the department for sex education. At the same time, it sought working alliances with other organizations. With the advent of the republic, reform of the penal code seemed to have come within reach. But it was not just the rapidly changing governing coalitions that destroyed these hopes and advances. It was also the personalities involved, their incompatible leadership claims, as well as strategic and objective differences that caused these alliances to fail. Subsequently, Hirschfeld and his allies founded the Cartel for Reform of the Law Governing Sexual Offenses. It incorporated neither the competing Community of Self-Owners nor the League for Human Rights, much to those organizations' chagrin. Instead, Hirschfeld, Hiller, and Linsert tried a political strategy that Hirschfeld had anticipated on a scientific level long before: including the demands of homosexuals in the broader canon of sexual reform—reform of marriage and divorce laws, laws governing abortion, procurement, prostitution, and pornography. He consequently sought to close ranks with the women's movement, the so-called lay organizations for birth control, marriage-law reformers, and similar organizations.

In 1927, the cartel proposed a much noticed alternative reform of the penal code. The legal principles it contained were not implemented until the West German penal code reforms between 1968 and 1972.

The goal of abolishing Paragraph 175 was nearly reached during the summer of 1929. The parliamentary committee for penal law recommended, with the vote of its chairman, that the section be expunged. "Plain" homosexuality between adult males (over twenty-one years of age) would then not have been subject to prosecution. Simultaneously, new so-called qualified offenses were defined, which meant that homosexual activity continued to be punishable, even more severely than before, especially homosexual prostitution. This reform also never became law because parliament was dissolved yet again. In preparation for the deliberations of the parliamentary committee on penal law, there were heated arguments in the committee regarding which strategy should be pursued. The majority were of the opinion that the names of experts who were "above suspicion" should be passed to the committee chairman by way of intermediaries. Hirschfeld counteracted this decision by sending the committee chairman the list of names on the SHC letterhead. This high-handedness gave rise to a "general accounting." Richard Linsert, an official of the KPD (Communist Party of Germany), which at that time strictly rejected any and all cooperation with the Social Democrats, composed an extensive exposé of Hirschfeld's alleged current and previous misconduct. Today, it is no longer possible to verify its accuracy. It is true that Hirschfeld asked his lawyer, Walter Niemann (1880–ca. 1937), to take legal action against the exposé, but he also resigned his chairmanship, and the committee moved out of the Institute for Sexual Science. Under its new chairman, Otto Juliusburger (1867–1952), a close friend of Hirschfeld's for many years, and later under Heinrich Stabel, it was only a shadow of its former self.

Scientific Journals and Associations

Two years after it was founded, the Scientific-Humanitarian Committee resolved to publish a journal and in 1899 appointed Magnus Hirschfeld as editor of *Jahrbuch für sexuelle Zwischenstufen* (Yearbook for Sexual Intermediacy). Twenty-three volumes of the yearbook appeared until 1923 (twenty-two published by Max Spohr in Leipzig). It remains today the most important German-language resource for research in the history of homosexuality and the homosexual rights movement. But the yearbook itself was only a vehicle for implementing the strategy of "through science to justice." Hirschfeld strove to embed the topic of homosexuality completely within the field of sexology, which was then taking shape. Thus in 1908, with the support of the SHC, he undertook the founding of the first professional journal in the field, the *Zeitschrift für Sexualwissenschaft* (Journal for Sexology). Coeditors were the Viennese ethnologist Friedrich S. Krauss (1859–1938) and the Leipzig gynecologist Hermann Rohleder (1866–1934). The journal survived for only one year and was then subsumed into the competing publication of the gynecologist Max Marcuse

(1877–1963), who published *Sexualprobleme* (Sexual Problems) until 1915.

In 1908, Hirschfeld also became a founding member of the Berlin Psychoanalytic Association, together with Otto Juliusburger, Heinrich Körber (1861–1927), Karl Abraham (1877–1925), and Iwan Bloch (1872–1922). Juliusburger and Körber were also active members of the SHC. His liaison with psychoanalysis did not last for long. In 1911, Hirschfeld parted ways when he had to admit that psychoanalysts did not share his view of homosexuality as inborn, and instead sought its causes in the psychological development of the individual.

He continued to seek out scientific allies. Thus in 1913 we find Hirschfeld among the founders of the first sexological professional organization, the Ärztliche Gesellschaft für Sexualwissenschaft (Medical Society for Sexology). Over the course of its existence, it had internal conflicts and changes in self-definition as a group, expressed in the various addenda made to its name: Medical Society for Sexology and Eugenics, . . . and Eugenetics, . . . and Genetic Research, . . . and Sexual Policy. The association also published a journal, again under the title *Zeitschrift für Sexualwissenschaft* (Journal for Sexology), edited by Albert Eulenburg (1840–1917) and Iwan Bloch. The same events repeated themselves. This journal too, on the decision of its publisher, was sold in 1919–20 to a competitor, a group of scientists surrounding Max Marcuse and Albert Moll. Thus Hirschfeld was left without a publisher. Also, during the second half of the 1920s, the membership of the Medical Society and the emphasis of its research had changed so much that Hirschfeld only rarely had a forum to present his findings. Meanwhile he created with his Institute for Sexual Science a new organizational form in which his scientific positions became predominant.

The World League for Sexual Reform

Completely in line with his project of integrating the particular issue of the criminal prosecution of homosexuals into a comprehensive social and sexual policy framework, Hirschfeld's last foundation was the World League for Sexual Reform, officially chartered in Copenhagen in 1928, but already operating in 1926–27. The World League, famous for its four large conventions (Copenhagen 1928, London 1929, Vienna 1930, Brno/Brünn 1932), modeled them on the International Convention for Sexual Reform on a Scientific Basis, which he had hosted at his institute back in 1921. The volumes of collected lectures given at the convention, however, reveal a dilemma: the issue most personally important for Hirschfeld, legal and social equality for homosexuals, was forced more and more into the background in contrast to counseling services, which focused on eugenic birth control, prosecutions for abortion, and sex education. In the end, after Hirschfeld's death, the contradictions between the ideas of middle-class and socialist sexual reformers led to the disbandment of the organization in 1935. Conventions planned in Moscow, Paris, and Chicago would never be realized.

The Institute for Sexual Science

Providing an organizational framework for the new discipline of sexology, in addition to the journals and professional organizations, was only logical, given that establishing a chair for it at a German university would have been impossible at the time. Thus Hirschfeld founded the Institute for Sexual Science in Berlin in 1919, using his own money. But he did not do it completely altruistically. In Imperial times, earning the title "Medical Councilor," just as with the title

"Commercial Councilor," was tied to some significant foundation or achievement benefiting the common good. (Some German princes awarded titles in exchange for payments to their state treasuries.) Following his official declaration early in 1918 of his intent to create the foundation, there was some back-and-forth before Hirschfeld received the title he had so longed for. True, it was not signed by the Kaiser, but still it was public recognition, not to be underestimated in the day-to-day social life of the upper middle class.

It took a little longer for official approval of the foundation. Permission was first granted at the end of 1918, then a second time in February 1919. The institute was finally able to open in July 1919. Hirschfeld had purchased the stately building In den Zelten 10 at the corner of Beethoven Street 3, located centrally near the Tiergarten, in 1918. It was called the Hatzfeld Palace, and was originally built for the violin virtuoso Joseph Joachim. Prince Hatzfeld, however, was not the seller, but a Count Ysenburg. Prior to this, Hirschfeld had already been residing and practicing medicine in the neighborhood: first at In den Zelten 19, then at number 16. The institute's operations soon proved to be so extensive that the neighboring house at In den Zelten 9a was also purchased and connected to the palace.

Staff Members

An institute may be led by one person, and Hirschfeld left no doubts about his leadership claims, but he couldn't do all the work himself, especially since his plans involved incorporating many different specialties in the Institute for Sexual Science. In addition to medicine, there was also biology, psychology and psychiatry, ethnology (including folklore), and anthropology. Research, teaching, and medical care were the three pillars of the institute's activity. Teaching encompassed programs on an academic level for students, continuing education for doctors, lawyers, teachers, visiting nurses, and police officers, as well as a broad spectrum of educational programs for the general public, including lectures, courses, evening counseling sessions, film programs, and the publication of journals. The emphasis of this work varied over the years and depended on the staff that happened to be employed at a given time. Ultimately, sexual policy and sexual reform were the permanent tasks as the spectrum of topics was continuously broadened.

Not everyone who worked at the institute briefly or for a longer period can be named here. As well, the destruction of the institute by the Nazis was so thorough that there are still gaps in our knowledge. Not all of the names have survived, biographical information is missing, and the time period of their staff participation or their staff assignments at the institute are not known. Often there are no known photographs.

Important medical staffers who worked with Hirschfeld at the institute, in the order in which they joined, were:

Dr. Arthur Kronfeld, M.D. and Ph.D., Psychiatrist and Psychologist (1886–1941; at the institute 1919–26)

Dr. Arthur Weil, M.D. and D.V.M., Neuroendocrinologist and Neuropathologist (1887–1969; at the institute 1920–22)

Dr. Bernhard Schapiro, M.D., Dermatologist and Endocrinologist (1922–1933)

Dr. Friedenthal, M.D., Anthropologist (1870–1943), at the institute 1922–24)

Dr. Ludwig Levy-Lenz, M.D., Gynecologist (at the institute 1926–33)

Dr. Max Hodann, M.D., Sex Educator (at the institute 1926–29)

Dr. Felix Abraham, M.D., Psychiatrist (1901–1938; at the institute 1928–33)

Also briefly on the staff were Friedrich Wertheim (Dermatologist), August Bessunger (1889–1943/44; Radiologist), Medical Councilor Eugen Littaur (b. 1870; Ear, Nose and Throat), Hans Graaz (1879–1953; Naturopathy), Franz Prange (1898–1969; Endocrinologist), Johannes/Hans Kreiselmaier (1892–1944; Gynecologist), and Berndt Götz (b. 1891; Psychiatrist).

Hirschfeld was able to obtain the services of Baron Ferdinand von Reitzenstein (1876–1929) as an ethnologist. Von Reitzenstein had previously worked at the Dresden Hygiene Exhibition, then did freelance work as an ethnological writer. He brought with him to the institute the journal he edited, *Geschlecht und Gesellschaft* (Sex and Society), as well as its supplement, *Sexualreform* (Sexual Reform). At first he was not able to move from Dresden to the institute as he had planned because of a lack of space. By the time the apartment intended for him in the building at In den Zelten 9a became available, von Reitzenstein had suffered a stroke from which he would never recover.

The offices of the Scientific-Humanitarian Committee were responsible for sexual reform and sexual policy at the institute, at first under the secretary of the committee, Georg Plock (1865–1930), "a former pastor with a history," as Kurt Hiller once wrote of him. Then, beginning in 1923, Richard Linsert took over, with support from his friend Peter Limann (1903–1941). When the SHC moved out of the institute in 1929, issues of sexual reform and sexual policy were handled by Wilhelm Kauffmann (ca. 1886–1933), a Prussian civil servant who had been removed from service because of a conviction under Paragraph 175. He directed the office of the World League for Sexual Reform, but was anything but the diplomat that would have been needed in this position.

Staff members who maintained the infrastructure of the institute included Friedrich Hauptstein, Hirschfeld's confidant and for many years administrative director; the librarian Arthur Röser; Hirschfeld's friend and life-partner Karl Giese, director of the archive; Ewald Lausch, medical assistant; various caretakers (often married couples); the cook, Miss Friedrichs; the housekeeper, Adelheid Rennhack (1909–2008); Aenne Diehl, domestic help; Helene Helling, the receptionist; Franz Wimmer, Hirschfeld's personal attendant; and Erwin Hansen, whom Christopher Isherwood mentions in his memoir *Christopher and His Kind*, the factotum.

Now and then temporary employees were engaged, especially in the offices of the SHC or as secretaries for Hirschfeld. These included Bruno Vogel and Günter Maeder (1905–1993). The domestic staff was sometimes complemented by people staying temporarily at the institute and too poor to pay for their rent or treatment. Rudolf R. (b. 1892), called Dorchen, is perhaps the best-known example.[42] Likewise Arno/Toni Ebel (1881–1961), who attained modest honors as a painter in the 1950s in East Germany, lived for one year in the basement of the institute.

Programs

During the first few years, the institute was mainly a place for academic research and training. Staff doctors offered seminars for students, conducted their own research, and published the results in scientific journals and books. Arthur Weil's research is especially noteworthy in this context. In a series of studies of the physical attributes of homosexuals, he attempted to provide proof of Hirschfeld's theory that homosexuality in men and women is accompanied by measurable physical attributes with values that lie between those found in heterosexual men and those found in heterosexual women. Arthur Kronfeld wrote his *Sexualpsychopathologie* (Sexual Psychopathology) and numerous essays on questions of sexual constitution and on psychotherapeutic treatment options for sexual disorders. Hirschfeld published the first chapters of his *Geschlechtskunde* (Sexology), which grew to comprise five volumes by 1930.

The second main activity of the institute was medical treatment of patients. During the first few years following the war this was mainly for venereal diseases. Gonorrhea and syphilis were commonplace, and their treatment much more difficult than it is today. Later, other problems became more important. Bernhard Schapiro, for example, frequently treated patients, both male and female, who suffered from the bodily effects of endocrine disorders. Erectile dysfunction was another reason to seek treatment at the institute. Men and women who wished to change their physical gender through surgery also came to the institute. Some instances of these so-called sex-change operations are described in the medical literature.

The third main activity of the institute was counseling and education. Besides the lectures and brochures, Hirschfeld and his staff also used instructional films. The best known of these is *Anders als die Andern* (Different from the Others; 1919), only a fragment of which has been preserved. Devices and methods for contraception and birth control were constantly recurring topics, and eventually the institute began offering fortnightly "Question Evenings" to provide information on these topics and they enjoyed great popularity. The institute's library was open to the interested public, and a guided tour of its collections came to be a tourist attraction in Berlin during the Weimar Republic. By the end of the 1920s, staffers of the Institute for Sexual Science were able to address themselves to the general public in two journals: *Die Aufklärung* (Enlightenment, that is, on sex education), edited by Maria Krische, and *Die Ehe* (Marriage), edited by Ludwig Levy-Lenz.

Prominent Location

The institute had five guest/patient rooms in the attic. Additionally, Hirschfeld's sister, Recha Tobias, rented rooms in her apartment. Among many who lived temporarily at the Institute for Sexual Science worthy of mention are the writers Walter Benjamin (1892–1940), Christopher Isherwood (1907–1986), Peter Martin Lampel (1894–1965), and Ludwig Renn (1889–1979); the philosopher Ernst Bloch (1885–1977); the dancer Anita Berber (1899–1928); and the "fake prince" Harry Domela (1904–ca. 1978). Together with his life companion Babette Gross (1898–1990), the KPD press officer and Member of Parliament Willi Münzenberg (1889–1940) lived from 1926 to 1933 in an apartment at In den Zelten 9a that was directly connected to the institute building and housed parts of the institute's collections in its hallways. Connected directly to the institute, the apartment was highly suited to meetings with conspiring visitors: did anyone notice which visitors went through which doors during a guided tour?

During the 1920s, the Institute for Sexual Science developed into one of Berlin's tourist attractions. The list of visitors is long and cannot even partly be presented here, but a few of the names are the Dada artist Til Brugman (1888–1958), the French writers André Gide (1869–1951) and René Crevel (1900-1935), W. H. Auden (1907–1973), as a friend of Isherwood's, Paul Krantz, who later became well known using the name Ernst Erich Noth (1909–1983), the painter Christian Schad (1894–1983), the filmmakers Sergei Eisenstein (1898–1948) and Ivor Montagu (1904–1984). Thea Sternheim (1883–1971) recounts in her diary how some Belgian friends cajoled her into visiting the institute. Even the aging Gerhart Hauptmann was seen there.

HIRSCHFELD'S FINAL YEARS

World Tour

ON NOVEMBER 15, 1930, Magnus Hirschfeld departed on a lecture tour to the United States from Bremerhaven aboard the *Columbus* alone. Karl Giese remained in Berlin. After his return to Europe, Hirschfeld made a detailed and vivid report of his adventures and experiences on this trip, though neglecting the first four months spent in the United States. *Die Weltreise eines Sexualforschers* (*Men and Women: The World Journey of a Sexologist*) appeared in Switzerland in 1933 and has been translated into English.

The first invitations were arranged by Harry Benjamin (1885–1987) in New York and Max Thorek (1880–1960) in Chicago. But it was already clear that this was just the beginning. On Christmas Eve 1930, in Atlantic City, Hirschfeld noted, "New York is probably just the beginning or one chapter of a world tour, since I plan to travel via Chicago and California to Tokyo and Shanghai, where I'm likely to receive or have already received lecture invitations. When I shall return to Germany depends on my well-being and on a few other factors."[43] Hirschfeld stayed for six weeks in New York, where he met writers and artists, doctors and scientists, did fieldwork in Harlem, the bathhouses, and at night court before continuing his journey to the Midwest. He visited Chicago and Detroit, visited relatives in Milwaukee, Wisconsin, and stopped by Niagara Falls along the way. The third stage in the United States was California, with lectures in San Francisco and excursions to Hollywood, Pasadena, San Diego, and as far as Mexico.

Initially, Hirschfeld presented his lectures in German, but his English appears to have improved enough on his trip that he began speaking publicly in English. Several lengthy interviews by George Sylvester Viereck* (1884–1962) appeared in the American press. Viereck later became infamous in the United States as an outspoken Nazi supporter. He also coined the phrase "The Einstein of Sex," an ingenious way of introducing the unknown Hirschfeld, since Albert Einstein had only recently arrived in California. Hirschfeld paid Einstein a visit in Pasadena.

During the course of his journey across the United States, Hirschfeld finalized his plan not to return directly to Europe but to accept lecture engagements in Japan and China and travel to Tokyo via Hawaii, departing from San Francisco. Because of his poor health from diabetes, friends in New

---

*George Sylvester Viereck was born in Munich, 1884 to an American mother and was the son of the prominent Social Democrat politician Louis Viereck. His father emigrated to the United States in 1896 and George came after in 1897. He became a published poet less than ten years later in 1904 and graduated from the City College of New York in 1906. A 1907 collection, *Nineveh and Other Poems* (New York: Moffat, Yard & Company, 1907), contained homoeroticism in the classical idiom then in vogue. A vampire novel dates from the same year. *Confessions of a Barbarian* (New York: Moffat, Yard and Company, 1910), in which he detailed travels through Europe and interpreted European culture for Americans, was a bestseller, and he became nationally known. He lectured on American poetry at Berlin University. He was married and had a son, Peter Viereck. He became interested in Germany and a proponent of the German cause in both world wars. As a journalist he interviewed many prominent people, including Sigmund Freud. He interviewed Adolf Hitler in 1923 and met him again in 1933. He was a prominent American Nazi and was imprisoned from 1942 to 1947 for failing to register with the United States as a Nazi agent. His prison memoir, *Men into Beasts* (Robbinsdale, MN: Fawcett Publications, 1952), details situational male homosexuality and rape, helping inaugurate gay pulp fiction. He died in Massachusetts in 1962.—*Trans.*

York and Chicago had repeatedly warned him of the strain any such trip would put him under, but Hirschfeld was not an obedient patient. In his records he made this notation:

> Especially the doctors in Chicago, first and foremost Dr. Thorek, made me so fearful and kept drilling into me the sentence "Don't go to the Orient" with all kinds of threats like "Coma diabeticum," gangrene, etc., that I should be in dread of if I did not take care of myself. It is certainly true ... that staying on a diet while traveling, in restaurants, hotels, dining cars and private homes where I've been invited, also aboard ship, is much more difficult than it is at home. Also true that the itching sometimes becomes rather intense, and causes a danger of infection because of the scratching.[44]

His own perception differed:

> Subjectively, I feel very well on this trip, certainly better than I've felt the past few years in Europe. The very painful and disabling nerve inflammation in my left arm is completely gone. Even the toothaches that bothered me so much seem to have disappeared. I feel fatigued only in a completely natural proportion to my level of activity, which is excessive, both by comparison to my normal activity level and for my age (partly because of inner restlessness). All my vital functions are working well—in short, I can't imagine that I am already a candidate for death (any more so than nearly anyone else). At the very least, I shouldn't like to think of myself as an invalid for life just yet.[45]

He needed the challenges of new experiences, and he needed an audience, which he no longer had in Germany, or had only under more difficult conditions:

Of course, there were other reasons besides the circumstances in Germany. For instance, a long-harbored yearning, after finishing the *Geschlechtskunde*, to have at least a year of "creative pause" follow upon all the hard labor. Also, a certain weariness with the movement. . . . And the continuing disappointments with the institute, the difficulty finding satisfactory support staff . . . together with the lack of harmony among those colleagues agreeable to me. . . .

One just wants out, with no clear idea of what is to come. Besides, the mood came over me, perhaps not quite to the extent now realized: "My sphere is the world"—not just Germany, not just Europe.[46]

In 1931, in this optimistic mood, Hirschfeld traveled through Japan. Then, based in Shanghai, he spent six weeks in China. In Shanghai he met Li Shiu Tong (Tao Li), a twenty-four-year-old medical student, who would accompany Hirschfeld, as his student and companion, on the further journey via the Philippines and Indonesia to Singapore, Ceylon, India, Egypt, and Palestine, and back to Europe. Hirschfeld noted at the beginning of October 1931 in Patna, India:

One of the greatest yields of my journey has been Tao Li, a well-bred young Chinese who has accompanied me for the last five months. His noble character, his intelligence, his unswerving loyalty and devotion have made this journey so much easier, it's extraordinary. It is his wish, and that of his father, that he should study medicine and sexology in Germany. I believe to have found in him the student I have sought for so long, one that I can form in my own image.[47]

Hirschfeld gave Li power of attorney over his possessions and manuscripts in the case of his death while traveling. Li was supposed to bring his ashes to Berlin and be able to remain at the institute as long as he saw fit.

The stress of traveling, especially the heat and humidity of the tropics, finally took its toll. During October and November of 1931, Hirschfeld was in Bombay, bedridden with malaria. "I had to regard it as a great good fortune that in areas where plague and cholera are everyday occurrences, I 'only' came down with malaria (fever of up to 105°)."[48] Relapses of malaria also prevented Hirschfeld from giving all the lectures he had planned in Egypt. He spent Christmas 1931, as the year before in America, at the seaside. "I'd like to see a Christmas tree, and so I'm taking Tao Li to the Bavarian Beer Hall, a sailors' bar in Alexandria."[49]

He was powerfully drawn to Palestine, the last important non-European stop on his tour. Hirschfeld was more impressed with the young people on the kibbutzim, experimenting with collective living, than with the historic sites of the Bible. He was skeptical about the possibility of finding a common way forward together with the Arab population.

Hirschfeld conceived of his tour as a sexological-ethnological study tour. Many of the objects presented to him, or acquired along the way, he shipped to the Institute for Sexual Science, including a stone phallus from Indonesia weighing a hundred pounds. In the introduction to *Weltreise eines Sexualforschers* (*Men and Women: The World Journey of a Sexologist*), published in 1933, he tried to summarize it: "Upon earth there are no two countries or peoples whose sexual institutions are completely identical." Yet these differences were not based on any dissimilarity of sexual attributes, which are the same among all peoples and have only individual differences. The diversity of sexual customs is contingent solely on all the manifold forms of sexual expression. Hirschfeld insisted that various customs have real origins, and that it was only in a later stage that, retroactively, symbolic and idealistic explanations for them were created. Since every people and every religion are inclined to view their own customs as the commandments of an objective, universally valid morality, it has not yet been possible for humanity to find "a coherent solution to the various sexual and romantic customs that would correspond in any way to the findings of sexual biology and sexual sociology." Hirschfeld saw the task of sexual ethnology this way: "Only an objective and scientific study of mankind, and of sex, can prepare the way for the complete realization of human sex rights."[50]

Exile and Death

Hirschfeld never returned to his institute with the proceeds from this trip. When he was in India, Hirschfeld began receiving warnings from Berlin that led him to doubt whether it would be advisable for him to return. The possibility of an imminent exile was quite plain by the autumn of 1931. But at this point the threats to life and limb were still distant and the institute remained open, though in a hostile environment. The Nazis were not yet in power.

When he arrived in Athens, Europe's quarrels caught up with Hirschfeld. He writes:

Hardly had I set foot again upon European soil on March 17 [1932] when the harassment began again; even in Athens, where I landed, there were immediately lies in the papers [imported from Germany], even more so in Vienna, and from Germany itself, threatening letters and printed threats ("we'll take care of him," "his time has run out"). Certainly, I don't lack for good company (Einstein!).

But that makes my situation, should I return home, seem even that much more horrendous. . . . I consider it beneath my dignity to live among a people who regard me as a "foreigner."

Me, when I've written so many works in German for Germans.
If Germany doesn't want me, I don't want it either.[51]

It was difficult for Hirschfeld to remain away. But he knew
enough not to set foot in the land of his forefathers again.
Li Shiu Tong traveled to Berlin alone and visited the former
domain of his teacher and friend while Hirschfeld remained
in Vienna.

The year 1932 was filled with restless activity for
Hirschfeld, repeatedly interrupted with periods of illness—
he suffered from malaria, diabetes, and a painful polyneuritis
that kept recurring. Furthermore, Hirschfeld suffered heart
attacks that caused him to fear his end was near. He went
for treatments at the spas in Karlsbad (Karlovy Vary) with
his old friend, the physician Leopold Hönig, and Marienbad
(Mariánské Lázně), but found little relief. Traveling restlessly
back and forth, Hirschfeld was concerned with completing
the manuscript for *Weltreise eines Sexualforschers* (*Men and
Women: The World Journey of a Sexologist*), preparing the
conference of the World League in Brno, and worrying about
whether the institute for Sexual Science could survive and
continue its work. His friends from Berlin and colleagues
from the institute visited him in Czechoslovakia both before
and during the Brno conference at which Hirschfeld tried
to engage the young Dr. Josef Weisskopf as a new physician
for the Institute. By the end of 1932 Hirschfeld was living in Zurich, where it was quickly becoming clear to him
that his life's work would largely be destroyed, and was in
grave danger. Since the summer, the National Socialist government in Prussia had been trying to revoke the nonprofit
status of the Dr. Magnus Hirschfeld Foundation, the institute's sponsor. They had an easy time of it, since the progress
and financial reports, required to be submitted annually, had
either not been done at all or inadequately. Hirschfeld was

Magnus Hirschfeld with his sister, Jenny Hauck, in Kolberg by the monument to their father, Hermann Hirschfeld. Dated August 3, [19]30.

Magnus Hirschfeld. Portrait postcard with dedication, "H[is] d[ear] sister Jenny. 12.XI.27" (November 12, 1927)

Christmas party for the children of staff and suppliers
in the home of Magnus Hirschfeld, 1917.

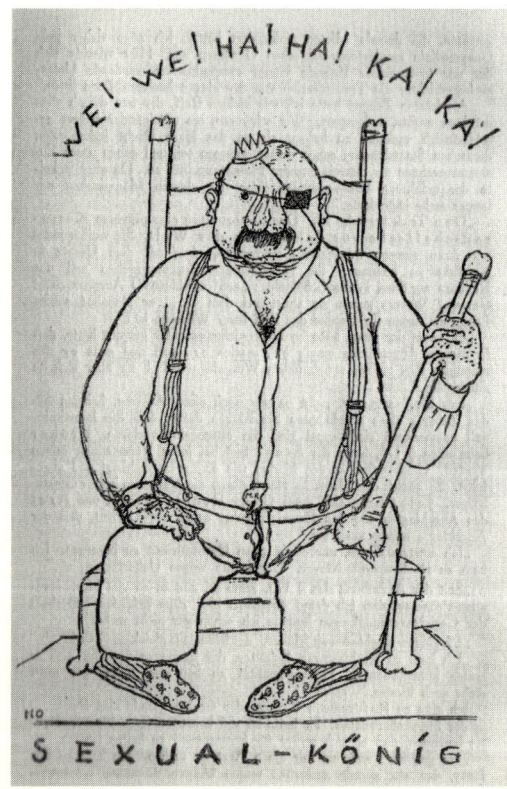

Satirical drawing by
Oskar Nerlinger
of Hirschfeld
as chairman of
the Scientific-
Humanitarian
Committee.

Portrait of Magnus Hirschfeld that the Nazis used to vilify him.

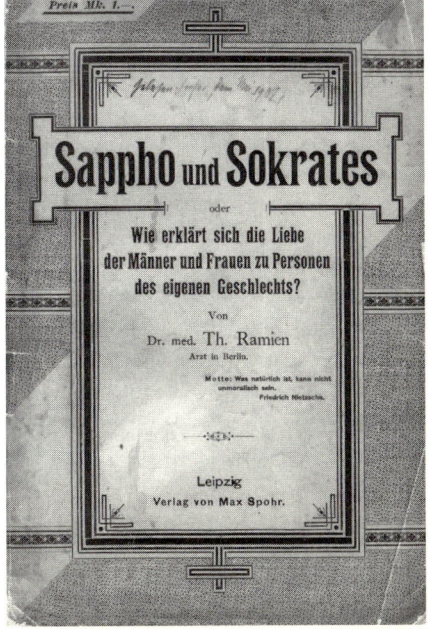

Title page of the brochure "Sappho and Socrates." This brochure, which Hirschfeld published in 1897 under the pseudonym "Th. Ramien," initiated his long-standing collaboration with the publisher Max Spohr in Leipzig.

The rooms of the Scientific-Humanitarian Committee in the Institute for Sexual Science.

INSTITUT FÜR SEXUALWISSENSCHAFT.

The main building of the Institute for Sexual Science.
(Picture postcard, undated.)

Magnus Hirschfeld with his colleague of many years,
Bernhard Schapiro, another physician at the institute,
in the Tiergarten (undated).

Karl Giese on the stage of the Ernst Haeckel Auditorium at the
Institute for Sexual Science.

Deployment of the National Socialist student fraternity in Beethoven Straße outside the institute. The plunder begins, May 6, 1933.

Photograph of the institute's library taken after the ransacking.
(*Archives of the Magnus-Hirschfeld-Gesellschaft, coll. Adelheid Schulz*)

Magnus Hirschfeld and Li Shiu Tong in Paris, 1933. Cover of the French illustrated *Voilà*, Nr. 119, dated July1, 1933.

A ball at the Institute for Sexual Science, not dated. Hirschfeld (second from right) holding hands with Karl Giese (in drag). The elderly lady in front on the left side is Karl's mother. (*Archives of the Magnus-Hirschfeld-Gesellschaft, Berlin*)

Brothers Hirschfeld. Left to right: Immanuel, Eduard, and Magnus, not dated. (*Archives of the Magnus-Hirschfeld-Gesellschaft, Berlin*)

Li Shiu Tong and Karl Giese in the front garden of the
Institute for Sexual Science, circa 1932.

Magnus Hirschfeld having coffee with his nephew, Günter R. Hauck, and
his fiancée, Gerda B. Marcuse, Berlin, 1930. (*Archives of the
Magnus-Hirschfeld-Gesellschaft, Berlin*)

Title page of the journal *Earth*. (*Archives of the Magnus-Hirschfeld-Gesellschaft, Berlin*)

Magnus Hirschfeld in the library of his institute, not dated. (*Archives of the Magnus-Hirschfeld-Gesellschaft, Berlin*)

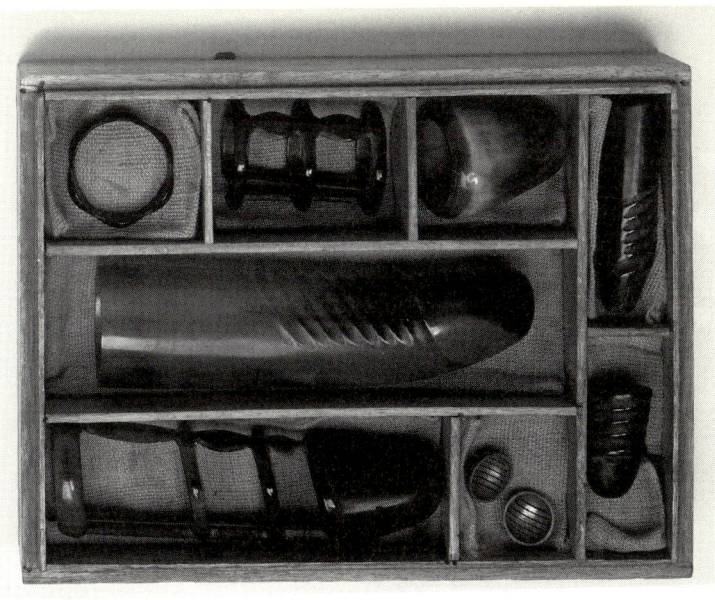

Japanese dildoes. One of the few saved items from the collections of the Institute for Sexual Science, currently on loan to be displayed at the Jewish Museum, Berlin. (*Archives of the Magnus-Hirschfeld-Gesellschaft, Berlin*)

Magnus Hirschfeld and Karl Giese, not dated, about 1932. (*Archives of the Magnus-Hirschfeld-Gesellschaft, Berlin*)

Prof. **Magnus Hirschfeld**
Europe's Greatest Sex Authority
"HOMOSEXUALITY"
Beautiful Revealing Pictures
Postponed to SUN., JAN. 18, DIL-PICKLE CLUB, 858 N. State St.

THE NEWBERRY LIBRARY

Advertisment for a Hirschfeld lecture in Chicago, 1931.
(*The Newberry Library, Chicago, Dill Pickle Club Records*)

Magnus Hirschfeld with his sisters, Jenny Hauck, Recha Tobias, and
Franziska Mann (left to right), at the beach in Kolberg/Kołobrzeg, not dated.
(*Archives of the Magnus-Hirschfeld-Gesellschaft, Berlin*)

Cover and two pages from Magnus Hirschfeld's German passport, showing the visa for his trip to the United States in 1930. (*Archives of the Magnus-Hirschfeld-Gesellschaft, Berlin*)

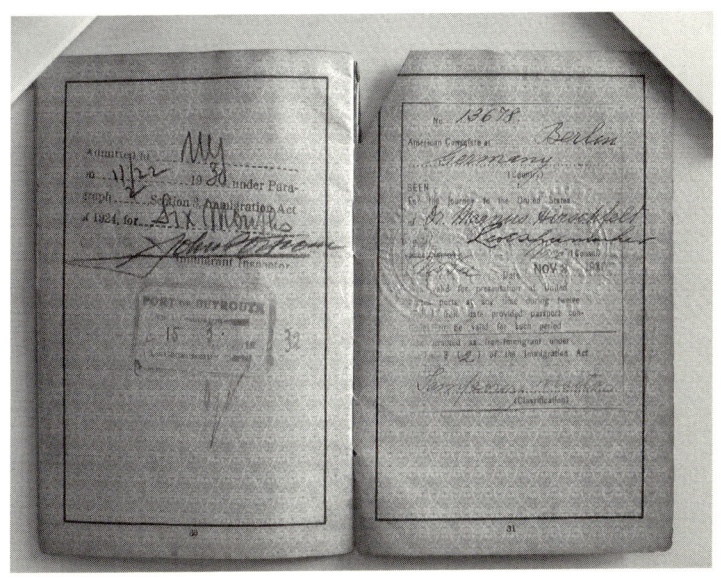

Magnus Hirschfeld and Li Shiu Tong in Nice, 1934. The reverse of this photo bears Hirschfeld's dedication to Dr. Edmond Zammert for his birthday, October 10, 1934: "Here's to many more years of our unified struggle for the Beautiful, Good and True!"

Magnus Hirschfeld appearing in court as expert witness, 1930.
(*Photograph by Leo Rosenthal, Landesarchiv, Berlin*)

"...amid the blazing torches and triumphant shouts of the Nazis,
the head of Magnus Hirschfeld was carried in effigy." (See Appendix 2)

Hirschfeld's grave in Nice with the portrait in relief by Arnold Zadikow. (*Photograph by Hans Bergemann, 2002*)

forced to recognize that he could no longer regard Friedrich Hauptstein, administrative director for many years, as "the rock upon which I built houses." Despite the institute's financial collapse, it appears that until April it was still possible to practice medicine there . Hirschfeld had relocated to Ascona, where Bernhard Schapiro sent several letters outlining plans for the future, including the possibility he might be able to stay on at the institute. He proposed preserving his employment opportunity at the institute by appointing a new "Aryan" medical director. This never came to pass.

On May 6, 1933, the institute was plundered by a horde of National Socialist physical education students. Portions of the library were thrown on a bonfire on the Opernplatz (Opera Square) on May 10, including Hirschfeld's bust, which had been skewered on a stick. A few days later, because his passport would soon expire and he could not risk applying for an extension at the German consulate in Zurich, Hirschfeld left Ascona together with Karl Giese and Li Shiu Tong. Hirschfeld spent his sixty-fifth birthday in Strasbourg and then sought refuge in Paris. "The French are kind to me, and friendly toward refugees."[52] Hirschfeld saw the newsreel film about the book-burning in a Paris movie theater.

The Nazi lawyer Dr. Hugo Vieck was installed as the administrator of the Berlin institute. He hurled terrible insults at the remaining staff, and offered to sell Hirschfeld portions of his own library and collections by way of his old friend Margarete Dost (1879–1956), threatening to destroy everything otherwise. The remaining holdings were sold at auction on November 14, 1933. Hirschfeld's entry in his testamentary notations reads:

Today, November 14, it has been three years since I left Berlin and never returned. Today, in my former home, begins the auction of my remaining books, materials, furniture—the last act (for now) of a fateful tragedy that comprises a terrible psychological martyrdom. Everyone was turned out of the house, even my sisters. The Bar Association took possession of the institute. I was completely stripped of all my rights, persecuted (a bounty put on my head) and insulted.[53]

Hirschfeld was indeed able to rescue some of the materials from the institute, whether by buying them back himself or through intermediaries like the Brno attorney Karl Fein (deported and murdered in 1943). With these remainders, Hirschfeld attempted to open a new institute for Sexual Science in Paris. For this, he required the help of Dr. Edmond Zammert (1861–1937), a friend and colleague of his brother Emanuel's from Upper Alsace. He was in possession of a French medical license, whereas Hirschfeld was not permitted to practice medicine in France. Karl Giese, who had moved from Brno to France in December 1933, was also included in the plans for the new Institute. He was supposed to organize what remained of the archive. But Giese was arrested in the late summer of 1934—"on account of an incident in a bathhouse," as Kurt Hiller later wrote—and subsequently deported from France. With some effort, Hirschfeld was able to deposit the materials rescued from Germany in the furniture storage warehouse of Bedel and Co. He gave one more lecture at the Sorbonne, which he saw as the high point of his stay in France, then with Li left for Nice, where he had spent the previous winter and had felt well near the sea. On February 1, 1935, he rented an apartment there.

If everything went according to my own wishes, I would find a place to live in my old age here or near Nice (on the Riviera in any case). My health is poor... at my age I have to forgo any great exertions, I have several good friends here (Ginsbergs, Hasenclever, Gordons, etc.), sufficient stimulation in my way of daily life, and above all, the sea and the sun as never-tiring, never tiresome stimuli.

Living another ten years under these conditions (maybe even live to see this Hitler-spook disappear,) if possible interrupted by a few trips: I don't really need anything more. The funds I have would allow it.[54]

He did not live to see the "Hitler-spook" disappear, but he was spared the fate that later befell the German emigrants in southern France. Hirschfeld died at midday on May 14, 1935, his sixty-seventh birthday, after having read all the letters from well-wishers with his grand-nephew, Ernst Maass, and Robert Kirchberger. Tao Li had just begun his studies in Zurich; Karl Giese was in Vienna.

Hirschfeld had left these instructions in the case of his death: "My wishes regarding my burial: cremation—music of Mendels[s]ohn and Schubert—no words from any clergy—remarks of friends, etc."[55] Not all of these wishes came to fulfillment. Although his body was cremated, against Jewish custom, a rabbi also spoke at the memorial ceremony. Hirschfeld was interred at the Cimetière de la Caucade in Nice. A simple vertical gravestone towers over the grave with a portrait of Hirschfeld in profile created by Arnold Zadikow (1884–1943). Like Hirschfeld, Zadikow was from Kolberg, and the commission for the gravestone contained in Hirschfeld's will was also an act of kindness for this exiled artist without means.

His Work

THE DOCTRINE OF SEXUAL INTERMEDIACY

HIRSCHFELD'S NAME IS FIRMLY linked with the concept of "sexual intermediacy," a summary description of his observations. Hirschfeld did not want his remarks to be understood as a "Theory of Sexual Intermediacy." A scientific theory provides an explanation for phenomena. By contrast, the doctrine of sexual intermediacy was conceived as a comprehensive description, a "principle of classification," an attempt to account for all such various phenomena and make them comprehensible in an ordered system.

The basic idea of the doctrine of sexual intermediacy is that all human characteristics, whether physical or psychological, occur in feminine or in masculine form—or, in exceptional cases, androgynously. In order to make the diversity comprehensible, Hirschfeld sorted these characteristics into four large categories:

—Sex organs
—Other physical characteristics
—Sex drive (sexual orientation)
—Other psychological characteristics

Masculine and feminine aspects of human attributes occur in all four categories and in an unending variety of mixtures and ratios. This results in the reality that a "full man" with exclusively masculine characteristics never occurs, and likewise a "full woman" with exclusively feminine characteristics is a product of fiction. In Wilhelmine Germany, when sex roles for "men" and "women" were far more defined than they are today, such a "dissolution of the sexes" must have seemed disturbing, even scandalous. Even so, Hirschfeld's ideas of what was "masculine" or "feminine" about a given characteristic was not essentially different from those current with his contemporaries. For him, the "masculine" element is active, creative, adventuresome, etc. The "feminine" element is passive, receptive, expectant. This classification is not connected to any super- or sub-ordination in the sense of superiority or inferiority. Rather, both elements are equally valid and equally necessary.

For each of the above mentioned four main characteristic categories of sexual intermediacy, there are groups of people who are distinguished by a mixture of masculine and feminine traits and thus can be presented as typical examples of the individual categories.

Sexual Intermediacy of Sex Organs

This category includes all persons whose sex organs cannot unequivocally be identified as male or female, or who have characteristics of both sexes. "Hermaphroditic" and "intersexual" are other terms with the same meaning. In close cooperation with the Warsaw professor Franz Ludwig von Neugebauer (1856–1914), Hirschfeld saw and examined many such persons. In many cases, Hirschfeld tried to help these individuals in overcoming everyday difficulties. After 1900, when the German civil code took effect, persons born with "ambiguous" sex organs were worse off with regard to treatment than they had been under the previously applicable Prussian provincial law. The German civil code provided that in such cases the physician or midwife decide the sex of the newborn child, effective for all time. Prior to 1900, this determination had been provisional. After reaching age eighteen, the affected person had the opportunity to decide whether he or she wished to live in future as a man or as a woman. Hirschfeld always viewed this ultimate self-determination on the part of the affected individual concerning his or her own life to be the more humane regulation, and he demanded again and again, though without success, that the German civil code be revised by reverting to the previous regulation. Although the law was without ambiguity, Hirschfeld pointed out that reality is ambiguous.

Sexual Intermediacy of Other Physical Characteristics

This group comprises a collection of various phenomena: women with beards or men with developed breasts being the most conspicuous. Any physical gauge or proportion can arise in this context: physical strength, excessive or deficient height, dimensions of the shoulders or hips, length of the teeth. All these were conceived as having masculine or feminine manifestations, with every possible intermediate stage.

Sexual Intermediacy of Sex Drive

For Hirschfeld, two main groups were subsumed under this category: homosexuality and metatropism. Though the first concept is still common today and requires no further explanation, the latter is a neologism of Hirschfeld's that did not gain acceptance in his own time and has been forgotten today. What did he mean by it? Hirschfeld had attempted to replace the terms sadism and masochism, which were then common. More precisely, he tried to integrate the forms of experience and behavior they designate into his concept of "masculine" and "feminine" manifestations of traits. Dominance and power in a sexual relationship he understood as "masculine," submissiveness and pleasure in pain as "feminine." The logical consequence of this conception, in contemporary terms, is that a sadistic man is merely taking his masculinity to excess, whereas a dominant or actively sadistic woman is metatropic. And vice versa, a masochistic woman is merely intensely feminine, and a masochistic man is a metatropic one.

Hirschfeld's research was centered on homosexuality, and in that context it is quite clear that the concept of sexual intermediacy is meant to help explain homosexuality. Hirschfeld and his colleagues attempted to identify traits of homosexuals, who a priori represent an intermediate type of sex drive, that were "typical of intermediacy." The researchers began with handwriting, moved on to body types, and went to the extent of measuring the length of individual limbs. The result, using a concept based on Ernst Kretschmer's doctrine of types, was something like a biological constitution of the homosexual, whose individual features could ultimately be traced back to the effects of specific hormone concentrations.

Sexual Intermediacy
of Other Psychological Characteristics

This category is also an aggregate that accommodates many varying traits. Hirschfeld considered handwriting, for example, as an expression of a masculine, feminine, or hybrid soul, just as bodily movements and facial expressions may be. Also, sartorial habits and requirements, to the extent they were not determined by external factors, such as in occupational clothing, were understood as an expression of an intermediate psyche. Thus male and female transvestites belong in this category. At the time the term "transvestite" referred not only to people who wanted to wear different clothes, but also those who felt they belonged to the opposite sex and wished to have the external features of their biological gender surgically altered. Today, we would refer to the latter group as transsexual or transgender. For transvestites, too, and especially for transsexuals, there were day-to-day legal difficulties for which Hirschfeld sought solutions. Wearing the clothing of the opposite sex in public was not illegal, but could be prosecuted as "disorderly conduct" or as "creating a public nuisance." Together with lawyer friends, Hirschfeld was successful in convincing the police, at least in Berlin, to issue "transvestite licenses" for this group. These were simple typewritten identification cards with a photograph and an official stamp that verified, for example, that the woman in possession of the card was known to "wear men's clothing."

Of course, it was also true of these large groups of "sexual intermediates" that they might display masculine and feminine features in various combinations of the four categories. For the individual it is always the predominance of one feature or another that is characteristic.

Hirschfeld's attempt to develop a scientific sexual classification system had an emancipatory political dimension. If every person is an "intermediate type," even so-called normal people, then ostracizing homosexuals, transvestites, and others loses its logic. Attempting to explain why a person is "that way" and not "another way" does not necessarily involve this concept.

The concept of sexual intermediacy as a catalogue of descriptions is open to explanations of where these various manifestations and behaviors come from, and what causes them. Hirschfeld believed in inborn, hereditary attributes that defined a person's "nature." In the day-to-day life of a society, the task is to help this nature achieve its rightful place, to let each person live "according to his or her own nature." Something that is "inborn," and is therefore "natural" or a "natural variation," is not governed by the free exercise of will by the individual, and therefore cannot be "unethical" or "immoral" or criminally punishable. From this sexual-political discourse, Hirschfeld attempted to garner arguments, in particular for the abolishment of Paragraph 175 of the German civil code pertaining to homosexuals.

During the years this concept was being developed, hormone research presented a promising approach toward explaining not only sexual preferences and behaviors but also characteristic physical traits. After the Viennese hormone researcher Eugen Steinach (1861–1944) succeeded in reversing the form of sexual behavior in rats and guinea pigs by implanting the opposite-sex gonads, Hirschfeld believed he was on the verge of a biological explanation of homosexuality. He hoped that in the near future evidence would be found in the testes of homosexual men and the ovaries of homosexual women showing that the hormones produced there differed from those in the organs of heterosexuals.

Unfortunately, this line of thinking led to Hirschfeld's participation in some crude experiments in the early 1920s. A succession of homosexual men who wanted to be cured of their sexual peculiarity were implanted with testes of heterosexual men. As might have been expected, some of the patients, after they recovered from the operation, thought they now had heterosexual needs. But it soon became evident that the implanted testicle tissue did not simply heal and begin producing hormones. Instead it was absorbed or even necrotized and had to be removed. The end result was a lateral or complete castration, with all the well-known consequences for the patient's physical and mental condition.

Around 1924 this method of "curing" homosexuals was conclusively discredited.

It is certainly striking that Hirschfeld apparently did not perceive the contradiction between his conception of homosexuality as natural and requiring no cure and these human experiments. At least, he never made mention of it. The fact that some of the patients on whom operations were performed were at high risk of suicide, and viewed this "cure" as their last and best hope, and that Hirschfeld as a physician could not and did not wish to deny them that hope, is only a superficial explanation. Had the experiments succeeded, what would have become of Hirschfeld and his fellow campaigners trying to achieve equal rights for homosexual men and women? Surely a social environment hostile to homosexuals would have resorted to mandatory reassignment or readjustment therapy.

Adaption Therapy

Hirschfeld had in fact developed a therapeutic concept for homosexuals (and other sexual intermediates) that was more likely to satisfy his political aspirations, and was more helpful for the persons affected. Astonishingly, he presented this concept to his medical colleagues only twice: once in 1914, secreted in his weighty tome *Die Homosexualität des Mannes und des Weibes* (Homosexuality in Men and Women; 2nd ed., 1920),[56] and then once again in an abridged version for the 1927 Psychotherapy Convention in Bad Nauheim. As simple and obvious as this procedure appears to us today, putting it into practice was precarious for physicians in Hirschfeld's era.

In brief, he invented the self-help group, or at least a prototype of it. Hirschfeld described his procedure under the rubric "adaption therapy" or "psychological milieu therapy."

In this therapy the physician must first determine whether the homosexual seeking consultation has any organic diseases and then examine his or her overall psychological condition. If these examinations show that no specific diseases exist, or that the diseases may be regarded as consequences of the rejection of homosexuality by the patient and/or by his or her social milieu, then the physician should inform the patient that homosexuality is not a disease and cannot be "healed." The physician should support the patient in strengthening his or her self-esteem and discuss the possibilities for shaping his or her life and sexuality without coming into conflict with the law. In Hirschfeld's era this presented a barrier to physicians. They could not simply recommend unlawful sexual conduct, especially since the danger of blackmail was well known. Thus they had to discreetly discuss what types of sexual behavior were not covered by the law (anal and oral sex was punishable), and how one could meet other homosexuals without exposing oneself to blackmail.

Hirschfeld viewed it as especially helpful if, at this stage, the physician could put the patient in contact with "intellectually superior like-minded persons," so that social isolation could be avoided and the patient given the opportunity of learning a way of living and behaving from "people like him or her." The Scientific-Humanitarian Committee provided Hirschfeld with just such a group, and it has been established that at the Institute for Sexual Science other "sexual intermediates" were provided with counseling and informed about groups and meetings of, for example, transvestites and transsexuals.

EUGENICS EDUCATION

ONE OF THE GREAT TOPICS in biology and medicine toward the end of the nineteenth century was how physical and psychological attributes are passed on to the next generation and whether we can have any influence over these hereditary traits. Advances in knowledge about hereditary regularities gave rise to the hope that a targeted application of eugenics might improve individual traits, or least, halt their purportedly unavoidable deterioration. "Degeneration" was the horror term of the era. Originating in psychiatry, the word quickly became a catchphrase in demographic politics. Hirschfeld, too, was convinced: "The quality of the individual genes . . . can be influenced either positively or negatively by external actions."[57]

Hirschfeld was interested in these actions. For example, alcohol can cause germ cell damage, so people should avoid alcohol, and alcoholics should not reproduce. Passing on damaged or "inferior" genes is damaging to the public health, and since, according to surveys cited over and over, people with purportedly "inferior" genetic constitutions reproduce more frequently than those with "good" genes, the entire nation was threatened with lapsing into degeneration and misery.

For homosexuality, too, Hirschfeld sought to secure its "natural" place in this scientific discourse. The homosexual person himself or herself is not sick or degenerate, but this may be a "trick" of nature to prevent damaged progeny in the subsequent generation. He made this argument repeatedly when discussing the question of whether homosexuals should marry. With the argument of social utility, he attempted to gain support for his political demands. This argument was not especially transformative, since homosexuals were still stigmatized as inferior.

In Hirschfeld's time, reproduction was seen not just as an individual right but as a social duty toward one's nation. This duty included having healthy progeny who, instead of becoming a burden on the community, would become useful members of society. The only point of contention regarding this duty was how it should be fulfilled, whether by government coercion or individual choice. Various alternative methods were discussed to give the state influence over human reproduction:

— Certificates of suitability for marriage (required or voluntary?);
— Sterilization or castration as prophylaxis and/or punishment;
— Information and education in counseling facilities (with or without the dispensing of contraceptives?).

Hirschfeld believed in the power of education. If people know what is right, what is useful for the individual and for society, they would adhere to it. He participated in the discussion on certificates of suitability for marriage as a representative of the Medical Society for Sexology and Eugenics at public hearings of the Imperial Council on Health in 1919–20. Hirschfeld was among those who rejected the duty to acquire a health certificate, but fully supported the voluntary exchange of information on the part of engaged couples. Thus it was entirely consistent that a marriage counseling center was affiliated with the Institute for Sexual Science. Under the direction of Hans Graaz, who was closely associated with the nudist movement, this center was also known as "Eugenic Counseling for Mother and Child." The records of this counseling center, the earliest of its kind in Germany, have not survived.

Hirschfeld departed from the fundamental standard policy of "informed consent" and viewed sterilization or castration as advisable compulsory measures for persons not capable of consent because of mental defects—in the terminology of the age, "mentally . . . stupid"—and for delinquent pedophiles.

In these cases, a "cure" was not foremost in Hirschfeld's thinking, but rather a protection for society. The belief that public health could be improved through eugenic measures was at that time especially widespread among left-of-center physicians. Even after the Nazis decreed a hereditary health law (the fact that it was aimed against "racial" and political undesirables did not escape his notice), he still did not regard eugenics as discredited in principle.

His Impact and Influence

WHEN HIRSCHFELD DIED, his Institute for Sexual Science had already ceased to exist. The Scientific-Humanitarian Committee had been dissolved and, because of their political differences, the remaining presidents of the World League for Sexual Reform, Norman Haire (1892–1952) and Jonathan Høegh von Leunbach (1886–1955), were not able and did not wish to keep it together. There no longer existed any institutions that might have been able to pass on either Hirschfeld's scientific legacy or his advocacy of social reform. Conditions in exile and during the subsequent war were not conducive to individuals trying to continue Hirschfeld's work.

HIS STUDENTS KARL GIESE AND LI SHIU TONG

AT THE END OF HIS LIFE, Hirschfeld had two remaining students to whom he entrusted his life's work: Karl Giese, who had lived with him at the Institute for Sexual Science, and Li Shiu Tong of Hong Kong, who had traveled with him. To them both he bequeathed the remaining holdings in his collections, the income from his publications and the remainder of his fortune, with the condition that it be used not for themselves but to found a new institute or, if that should not be possible, for the purposes of "our movement." Neither heir was able to fulfill his bequest.

After the institute was destroyed, Karl Giese fled to Czechoslovakia and lived in Brno in deprived circumstances. At the end of 1933, he lived for some time with Hirschfeld and Li in Nice and Paris. After his deportation from France, he stayed in Vienna and Brno. He had not graduated high school, which might have qualified him for vocational training, or even study at a university. It was ordained (by Hirschfeld) that he should prepare himself for the baccalaureate, but after Hirschfeld's death this was not possible for him for financial (and probably psychological) reasons. His friends from the World League, Norman Haire and Ellen Bækgaard, who had supported him heretofore, wrongly assumed that he had access to money for his studies from the inheritance and stopped their payments. Despite considerable efforts on the part of Brno attorney Karl Fein, Giese was not able to take possession of the items and funds intended for him from Hirschfeld's estate. "The bank where a safe deposit box, the contents of which are unknown, is located requires a document that in truth may only be obtained from the German Embassy, which all of us have reason to avoid," wrote Giese in the summer of 1935 to Max Hodann in England. It is not known whether Giese, apart from a few personal mementos, was subsequently in possession of any portion of the estate. He took his own life in Brno in 1938.

Li Shiu Tong did not complete his medical studies, which he began in Zurich in the summer semester of 1935, nor did he complete his subsequent studies in political economics. In Zurich he made the acquaintance of the English writer Robert Hichens (1864–1950), who based the character of Kho Lin in his novel *That Which Is Hidden* (London, 1939) on Li, and made Li's relationship with Hirschfeld a theme in fiction.

Li left Zurich in 1940 for the United States, studied at Harvard until 1944, worked briefly at the Chinese Embassy in Washington, D.C., and then returned to Zurich in 1945, where he first studied medicine and then political economics, again without earning a degree. Since he came from a wealthy family, earning a living was not urgently necessary. In 1960, he returned to Hong Kong. From there, he emigrated to Vancouver, Canada, in 1974, where his younger brother and several other members of his family had settled. In 1993 Li Shiu Tong died in Vancouver. In addition to personal mementos, his estate included books once owned by Hirschfeld, which Li had always kept with him, and probably Hirschfeld's travel diaries. From the few written records of Li that have come down to us, it is clear he felt an obligation as Hirschfeld's student to continue Hirschfeld's work but was overwhelmed by the task. He never wrote the book about Hirschfeld's teachings, and his own travel memoir, which Hichens urged him to write, never came to be. A portion of Li's estate, literally rescued from the trash heap of history by a young Canadian named Adam Smith, could be returned to Berlin with the support of the Stiftung Neue Synagoge Berlin, Centrum Judaicum.[58] A few years ago, the Magnus Hirschfeld Society, with the support of many friends, was able to acquire from the Li family the books from Hirschfeld's estate. Other personal mementos of his estate remain in the possession of his family in Hong Kong and Vancouver.

The remainder of Hirschfeld's estate is still missing, including the items and materials that were sold at auction in 1933 and which Hirschfeld did not reacquire. No collection voucher remains for the items deposited at the storage facilities of Bedel & Co. in Paris. Another part of his estate, in Nice, initially fell into the hands of unauthorized persons before it was handed over to his family, contrary to the terms of Hirschfeld's last will and testament. Recently, family members donated a large number of letters and photos to the Magnus Hirschfeld Society, and they are now preserved in the society's archive. Somehow, on a path that can no longer be reconstructed, a set of documents from the erstwhile institute found their way to Alfred Kinsey's Institute at Indiana University in Bloomington and are preserved there as the "Hirschfeld Scrapbook." Now and then, individual volumes from the institute's library show up in used and rare book shops. In recent years, German libraries began researching acquisitions that occurred during the Nazi period or just after it, work not yet completed. The Central and Regional Library of Berlin has already found one book from the library of the former institute and presented it to the Magnus Hirschfeld Society.

THE EXILES: HODANN, SCHAPIRO, HILLER, AND WEIL

AMONG THOSE WHO HAD worked together at the institute, it was the physician and sex educator Max Hodann who attempted to establish a similar institution during his period in exile in England, partly to help ensure his own future. Despite Hodann's great commitment, his plans did not succeed, even though he went to great pains, not simply out of consideration for English sensibilities, to avoid any and all association with homosexuality. He had to leave England at the end of 1935.

The dermatologist and endocrinologist Bernhard Schapiro, who had taken Swiss citizenship while attending university in Switzerland, was able to escape to Zurich with his family. There, and later in the United States and Israel, he took up again the type of specialized work he had done at the institute, but limiting it to the framework of his own medical practice.

The writer Kurt Hiller, who had campaigned alongside Hirschfeld as a member of the Scientific-Humanitarian Committee and was its last vice chairman, also survived in exile. From London, he commented critically on the attempts, which quickly failed, to found new similar organizations in Germany during the late 1940s and early 1950s. In the Swiss homosexual journal *Der Kreis* (The Circle) he paid tribute to Hirschfeld's work. When he returned to Hamburg from London, Hiller drafted and dispatched a petition in the spirit of the earlier SHC petition. These militant beginnings were not fated to succeed.

Arthur Weil, who had emigrated to the United States in 1923 and found a position as a neuropathologist at Northwestern University near Chicago, made contacts with members of the homosexual rights movement, which was beginning to develop in the United States during the 1950s, and also traveled to the first international convention in Frankfurt am Main in 1954. We do not know whether he made proposals at the convention for continuing a Hirschfeldian approach.

THE WORK OF REMEMBERING IN GERMANY

IN WEST GERMANY, after several failed organizational attempts in the early 1950s, the memory of Hirschfeld had been nearly completely obliterated. Sexology, which had been reestablished as an academic discipline after the war, initially drew on psychiatric theories, though that was not enough to obscure its origins in Nazi-era science. Later, sociological approaches were imported from the United States, though no one took notice that Alfred Kinsey had drawn on Hirschfeld's earlier studies of the proportion of homosexuals in various population groups.

The Dresden physician Rudolf Klimmer (1905–1977) was probably the last researcher who stood completely in the tradition of Hirschfeldian publishing. Immediately following the war in the Soviet Zone of Occupation, and later in East Germany, he attempted to influence legislation in a Hirschfeldian sense. His book *Die Homosexualität als biologisch-soziologische Zeitfrage* (Homosexuality as a Contemporary Question for Biology and Sociology), however, could only be published in West Germany (three editions from 1958 to 1965).

The Munich medical historians Werner Leibbrand (1896–1974), who had known Hirschfeld in Berlin, and Annemarie Leibbrand-Wettley (1913–1996), who became interested in Hirschfeld in the 1960s, were influential in generating a dissertation topic for Ralf Seidel. His 1969 dissertation makes clear that Hirschfeld's writings at that time were scarce in German university libraries. For non-academics, there remained available only overhauled continuations of *Sittengeschichte des Weltkriegs* (*The Sexual History of the World War*) (New York, 1934) and the volume compiled by Arthur Koestler (1905–1983) and edited by Norman Haire, *Sexual Anomalies and Perversions* (London, 1936), marketed in a German translation as erotic literature for many years at Beate Uhse, a German sex shop chain.

At the end of the 1960s a third homosexual rights movement began in Germany that was interested in its predecessors, and the silence was broken. Since 1982, the Magnus Hirschfeld Society has striven systematically to collect the remaining memories and make them available again. It would be another twenty years before the parties in the German parliament could bring themselves to declare the convictions of homosexuals under Nazi law an injustice and to rehabilitate those condemned, most of whom, of course, were no longer living. To commemorate these individuals, to research the history of homosexuals and their persecution, and to research the legacy and historical significance of Magnus Hirschfeld, the Magnus Hirschfeld Federal Foundation was created in the autumn of 2011 and endowed with 10 million euros from the budget of the Federal Ministry of Justice. Since 2012, the foundation has been able to use the interest from this endowment to support research and education projects meant to counteract discrimination against lesbians, gays, bisexuals, and transgender persons.

Epilogue—
Magnus Hirschfeld in North America

LIKE MANY FAMILIES in Pomerania, now Poland, the Hirschfelds had historical connections to the United States. One branch of the family emigrated to Illinois in the 1840s. They also had relatives in New York, which is where Magnus Hirschfeld supposedly held his first public lecture at the end of 1893 or the beginning of 1894. His topic was naturopathy, or natural medicine.

One of Magnus Hirschfeld's uncles on his father's side, Eduard, emigrated to California in 1850, at the time of the Gold Rush. Apparently he found his fortune there, since he was able to purchase return passage to Europe in first-class in 1857. Unfortunately, Eduard Hirschfeld drowned when the ship went down off the South Carolina coast.[59] Magnus Hirschfeld memorialized him:

> Hermann Hirschfeld [Magnus's father] had a favorite brother called Eduard. Intellectually gifted, but unsettled, this brother had emigrated years earlier to California. He wanted to bring nourishment, physical but especially

spiritual, to the many German emigrants who had gone to try their luck as gold miners. After successful and happy years in the city of San Francisco, which he had helped to found, he was overcome with homesickness and a longing to see his mother. But on the voyage, on the Atlantic Ocean, a fire broke out on board the ship, which was called the *Central America*. Fellow passengers reported that Eduard certainly could have saved himself and reached a nearby island, as they had. But he considered it his duty first to help all the others, namely the women and married men ,into the lifeboats, until it was too late to save himself and he went down with the sinking, burning ship.[60]

Magnus Hirschfeld visited North America twice himself: the first time as a young man just finished with his medical degree, the second time on a lecture tour at the invitation of his American colleagues. According to his own account, he paid for his 1893–94 trip with fees for writing newspaper reports about the World's Fair in Chicago, although not one of these reports has been identified. Presumably, they appeared in the *Kolberger Zeitung für Pommern* (Kolberg News for Pomerania), where his father had had a weekly column. Only a very few issues of this paper survived the Second World War.

The real reason for this first trip to the United States was to visit his brother Emanuel, who had recently become chief physician at the Sacred Heart Sanatorium, a rehabilitation institute, in Milwaukee. The sanatorium was a Kneipp naturopathic facility operated by nuns of the Franciscan Order of St. Joseph. In 1900, Emanuel Hirschfeld and W. R. Whitacker jointly founded the North Shore Health Resort in Winnetka, Illinois, sixteen miles north of Chicago. It was an elegant clinic for the upper classes, and for a time was considered "chic." Today it might be referred to as a "wellness retreat," or something similar. In 1913, Emanuel Hirschfeld published an advice book on healthy living called *The Heart and the BloodVessels: Their Care and Cure.* It was reprinted four times by 1916.

After his pharmacy business in Hamburg failed, Magnus's second brother, Eduard, also tried his luck in the United States at the beginning of the twentieth century. But his ventures there did not succeed either, and he died young in 1910.

Hirschfeld's favorite cousin Agnes Mann traveled back and forth between the old and new worlds. She studied dentistry at Northwestern University in Evanston, Illinois, in the early years of the century and returned there in the 1920s after having practiced for years in Bremen and Berlin. In her retirement she moved to Los Angeles, where she died in 1958.

More distant Hirschfeld relatives escaped the growing threat of German fascism by coming to the United States, such as his great-nephew Ernst Maass, who later became librarian at the United Nations in New York, and his cousin-in-law Leo Meyer, who until 1938 was the chief executive of Bijenkorf, the famous department store in Amsterdam. Meyer later lived in Los Angeles.

Hirschfeld's second visit to North America came at the height of his career, at the end of 1930 and the beginning of 1931. The encounters he experienced on this lecture tour, which took him from New York via Detroit, Chicago, and Los Angeles to San Francisco, did not make it into his book *Die Weltreise eines Sexualforschers* (*Men and Women: The World Journey of a Sexologist*). A few letters, from which some passages were printed in German newspapers, and brief notes Hirschfeld made in the handwritten diary-like *Testament: Heft II* (Testament: Notebook II) survive.[61] In New York, Hirschfeld spoke several times at the Labor Temple, as well as to both medical and psychoanalytic societies. The German-language *New Yorker Volkszeitung* (New York People's Newspaper) carried extensive reports on these lectures. He met Judge Ben B. Lindsey,* on trial for disorderly conduct as a result of his confrontation with Bishop Manning. He met Langston Hughes and James Weldon Johnson at afternoon tea with Carl Van Vechten. He spoke with the prominent attorneys Arthur Garfield Hays and Clarence Seward Darrow; and with Anita Loos he went to see "pornographic films." Hirschfeld was in turn filmed for the newsreels. On December 22, 1930, the *New York Times* reported on a newsreel program at the Embassy Theatre†: "Magnus Hirschfeld, founder of the Institute of Sexology, discusses his theories . . ."[62] Sadly, this film has been lost.

In addition to his personal connections, Hirschfeld had professional contacts in the United States. Arthur Weil, an

---

*The Honorable Ben B. Lindsey (1869–1943), a Colorado judge, and the Reverend William T. Manning (1866–1949), Bishop of the Diocese of New York, Episcopal Church, USA, were involved in a public dispute when Hirschfeld was visiting New York. Lindsey was well known for advocating "companionate marriage," which would allow young people to try out living together before marrying to determine whether they were compatible, on the condition that they agree not to have children. Manning condemned the idea as a license for premarital sex. In December 1930, Lindsey responded to a sermon by Manning at the Cathedral of Saint John the Divine in Morningside Heights, interrupting the service, and demanding an opportunity to rebut Manning's charges. Lindsey was arrested on charges of disorderly conduct.

†The Embassy Theatre, at 1560 Broadway, between West 46th and 47th Streets in Times Square, was opened in 1925 by Loews, Inc., as a movie theater for high society. It was unusual for being operated almost entirely by women, with the heiress Gloria Gould as manager. It was sold to Guild Enterprises in 1929. On November 1 of that year it adopted an all-newsreel program, which continued into the late 1940s. —*Trans.*

early staff member at the Institute for Sexual Science, immigrated to the United States in 1923, after having studied there the previous year. He first worked in Chicago, then in New York. Max Thorek, also practicing in Chicago, was a friend of Harry Benjamin, who later became famous for his research on "The Transsexual Phenomenon." Benjamin had been in close contact with Hirschfeld and the Institute for Sexual Science since the early 1920s, and was well informed about the first sex-change operations performed there.[63] The physician and sexologist William J. Robinson had studied in Berlin and returned to Germany repeatedly during the 1920s. The report he wrote about his visit to the Institute for Sexual Science has been reprinted as an appendix.[64]

In New York, Hirschfeld had a peculiar—and from today's perspective quite irritating—relationship with George Sylvester Viereck, who would later be condemned as a Nazi spy. Hirschfeld had been a friend of George Sylvester's father, the Social Democratic politician Louis Viereck. Hirschfeld remained close to the family, especially to George Sylvester, after his father died. George Sylvester Viereck did advance publicity for Hirschfeld's tour through the United States and accompanied him on it. The sobriquet "The Einstein of Sex" was his invention. He had already published a portrait of Hirschfeld in his book, *Glimpses of the Great*. But Hirschfeld was not blind to George Sylvester Viereck's sympathy for the Nazis. In October 1933 he wrote to him:

> For my part, I will not reject you; for I know your mentality all too well, and foresaw that you would not be able to resist Hitler's mass suggestion. I assume that you received my letter warning you against this illusive deception and of the dangers that may arise both for you and your American ventures because of it. . . .

I have written a small book called *Racism*, and I hope it will convince you. . . .

Nor do I believe, as you claim, that the world must undergo a Bolshevist or Fascist phase. On the contrary, in my opinion it is the three great democracies—France, England and America—that thus far, especially culturally, have proven to be a solid block; and that we must strive to do everything, as world citizens, to keep alive this hope for the future. And after all, you're one yourself, especially since you're both a German and an American.[65]

Completely different types of Americans among Hirschfeld's acquaintances included the women's rights advocate and anarchist Emma Goldman. With Margaret Sanger he shared an interest in birth control, and he visited her while he was in New York; he also had several encounters with her representative in Berlin, Agnes Smedley. Jan Gay (originally Helen Reitman), later well known as a lesbian activist, had stayed at the Institute for Sexual Science as a guest. Her interviews with lesbian women in Berlin, Paris, London, and New York were published by Dr. George W. Henry, under his name.[66] Elsa Gidlow wrote about her visit to the institute in her autobiography.[67] Another visitor was Gavin Arthur—actually Chester Alan Arthur III, a grandson of the twenty-first president of the United States. In his later work as an astrologist in San Francisco, Arthur included homosexual and bisexual life paths in his astrological readings. His book *The Circle of Sex* (1962) contains ideas similar to Hirschfeld's description of sexual intermediacy.

Early attempts to organize homosexual men in the United States, including Henry Gerber's 1924 Society for Human Rights in Chicago, were inspired by Adolf Brand's Gemeinschaft der Eigenen (Society of Self-Owners) and by Friedrich Radszuweits Bund für Menschenrecht (League for

Human Rights), even though Henry Gerber (1892–1972), who had been in Germany as a U.S. soldier during the First World War, was familiar with Hirschfeld and the Scientific-Humanitarian Committee. Whether Hirschfeld met Gerber, either in New York or Chicago in 1930–31, is not known. From his notations in *Testament: Heft II*, it is apparent that Hirschfeld met with many homosexual men and women in the United States, and undertook studies of their subculture, but there is no indication of any organizing activity.

At the beginning of his trip—in New York, Newark, Detroit, and Chicago—Hirschfeld lectured in German. On the long rail trip to the West Coast, he improved the English he studied in school to the point that he could hold lectures in English in Los Angeles and San Francisco. He noted in Honolulu, after he had left the United States and was on his way to Japan, "With regard to the 'Lectures,' I'm especially pleased that by really immersing myself in the English language I now (at least theoretically) can make my teachings comprehensible to 250 million more people than I could before."[68]

Striking differences are found in American reporting on Hirschfeld's lectures. In the New York German-language press, there were extensive accounts of his lectures on homosexuality. But of the reports and interviews that have so far come to light in English-language papers nationwide during his three-month U.S. tour, nearly all focus on his advice to rely on scientific partner selection and eugenic marriage counseling rather than love to find one's life partner. In some quarters these notions were reported as an entertaining curiosity.

In interviews Hirschfeld made a number of critical comments about American culture based on his experiences on the tour. As a sex researcher, he was put off by the blatant prudishness regarding sexual issues. With regard to

Prohibition, then in effect, the tour brought about a change in his attitude. Hirschfeld was opposed to alcohol and had published several critical articles both before and after the turn of the century about its harmful effects. But experiencing Prohibition in practice, which he did in the United States, made it clear to him that compulsory measures only achieve the opposite of what is intended. He subsequently spoke out against government prohibitions as a means to create healthy or moral behavior in people. He took a similar standpoint on eugenics. Eugenics was, in the argot of the time, "improving our racial stock." For this reason, Hirschfeld was especially interested to learn more about the experiments in California with forced sterilization of the "mentally ill" and the "mentally deficient," and to meet Americans who were active in the eugenics movement. Thus it is no coincidence that he went to Pasadena and visited Paul Popenoe and Ezra S. Gosney.

Hirschfeld also had a critical perception of the living conditions of African Americans, but as far as we know at present did not express these views publicly. Later, in April 1933, he made a notation in his *Testament: Heft II* about recent developments back in Germany: "The date of the Jewish boycott—April 1, 1933—will live on, not just in Jewish history! Recently, the humiliation and degradation of the Jews has made greater progress from day to day and is now nearly greater than that of the Negroes in America."[69]

When Hitler assumed power in Germany, it was clear that Hirschfeld would have to find a new home. He had a few options: go to China with his student and life partner Li Shiu Tong, remain in France, or accept invitations to relocate to the United States. He decided on the South of France. At the age of sixty-seven, he no longer felt up to the fast pace and the demands of a new professional life in the United States. Hirschfeld never regretted this decision, up until his early death in 1935. The Nazis later murdered many of his fellow German refugees in France, and would have done the same to him.

Some of the papers from Hirschfeld's estate later made their way to North America. The Kinsey Institute for Research in Sex, Gender and Reproduction possesses what is known as the Hirschfeld Scrapbook, which Alfred Kinsey acquired from an unknown person. It primarily contains documents collected by Carl Hoeftt, a Hamburg member of the Scientific-Humanitarian Committee. Apparently these papers were originally in a different order, and recompiled after the plundering of the Institute for Sexual Science and/or during the odyssey of flight and exile.

Li Shiu Tong kept everything Hirschfeld left him, took it with him on all his journeys, and conserved it until his death in 1993 in Vancouver, British Columbia. From this estate portion, Adam and Nancy Smith of Vancouver rescued a suitcase stuffed with documents and presented it to the Magnus Hirschfeld Society in 2003. The society later was able to acquire from Li Shiu Tong's family several cases full of books from Hirschfeld's and Li's estates.

Hirschfeld's great-nephew, Ernst Maass, who as a young man left Germany like his uncle, was in Nice when Hirschfeld died. He took many family papers, letters, and photos from Hirschfeld's estate to Palestine, and later to the United States. His son Robert Maass has donated all these documents to the Magnus Hirschfeld Society.

With support from researchers in North America many other sources may be discovered. Among the papers of George Sylvester Viereck are presumably many letters from Magnus Hirschfeld and from his sister, the writer Franziska Mann. The lives of his brothers, Emanuel Hirschfeld (Winnetka) and Eduard Hirschfeld (Chicago), have not yet been researched. Nor has the life of his cousin Agnes Mann or those other relatives who emigrated. It was their progeny who accompanied Hirschfeld on his travels through the United States.

Appendix 1

THE INSTITUTE OF SEXUAL SCIENCE: THE ONLY INSTITUTION OF ITS KIND IN THE WORLD
William J. Robinson, M.D.

She was a striking looking woman, and she did not wear her hair bobbed. To wear abundant masses of hair is now a sign of independence, just as a few years ago the demonstration of an independent spirit was a bobbed head. I entertained myself with her on various subjects, the weather, theater, Hindenburg's election and its effects on France and other European countries—and all the time I did not suspect that there was anything wrong with my new acquaintance. And then she said: You evidently don't suspect that I am a man? Under any other circumstances I would have had a shock or would have felt greatly embarrassed. But here, where I write these notes, "she" you learn after a while not to be surprised at anything. Yes, "she" was a man, a perfect man anatomically, yet his—or should I say her—soul was the soul of a woman. In every respect. And I would challenge any of our sleuths or vice-squaders to detect that she-he was a man when she-he walked in the street dressed in female clothes. The abundant mass of hair was of course a wig. And when asked why go to the extra trouble of wearing a wig when so many women wear now their hair cut short like men, the answer was that bobbed hair did not seem to him (her) feminine enough; he disliked bobbed heads, and he insisted on wearing his hair "like a true woman."—I had here before me a perfect type of Transvestite. It is hardly necessary to explain to the readers of THE CRITIC AND GUIDE the meaning of the term, but I shall do so for the benefit of new readers to whom the word may be unfamiliar. A Transvestite is a person who has an irresistible desire to wear the clothes of the opposite sex. And just as there are men who must wear female clothes, so there are women who feel utterly wretched and miserable unless they can put on male clothes. The term was coined by Dr. Magnus Hirschfeld and has now gained universal currency.

Some of the transvestites are not satisfied unless they can change their apparel completely so as to be taken for members of the other sex. Some, however, are satisfied with half-way compromises. Thus, certain male transvestites will satisfy themselves with wearing fine female undergarments, long silk stockings, a fine silk petticoat (under the trousers, of course), etc. This permits them to attend to their business, not to run the risk of arrest, and still feel that they have some of the female belongings on them.

With the compromises in dress that some female transvestites make we are all familiar. Then others make compromises as to time. That is, they will be dressed all day, while in their store, office, school or factory, in their normal clothes, i.e. clothes belonging to their sex, but in the evening when in the privacy of their home, they will quickly discard their habilements and deck themselves out in the clothes of the opposite sex. Many of the transvestites (those who are not homo-sexual; I'll touch upon that point presently) are married and in many cases their spouses help them to indulge in their ... let us say, peculiarity.

I just referred to transvestites who are not homosexual, it is an error commonly made by the uninformed, to confuse transvestites with homosexuals, to hold the two as synonymous. Not at all. Transvestites may be homosexual, and homosexuals may be transvestites: but just as there are homosexuals who are not in the least transvestites, so are there transvestites who are not at all homosexual, but strongly heterosexual. Their abnormality expresses itself only in the urge towards clothes of the other sex.

And right here I want to touch upon an important point. As is well known, our, in many respects blessed, country, is the most liberal in the world in regards to sexual abnormalities. Nowhere in the world are the slightest sexual peculiarities so viciously prosecuted, so brutally punished as they are in our United States. Nowhere has the blackmailer such a rich field, nowhere does he reap such a rich harvest.

I discussed with one of our liberal lawyers the case of a man who was given six months in prison because he was discovered wearing female attire. At the trial his lawyer pointed out to the judge that the defendant had the urge from his childhood, from the time he was seven or eight years old. But the ignorant judge who had never heard of such a thing as transvestitism ruined the man's life by sending him away for six months. And the "liberal" lawyer with whom I discussed the case found the sentence perfectly proper. "We cannot permit crazy whims and vices to flourish." Is an urge which exists in a man from his early childhood and which leads him to commit suicide if he is unable to satisfy it just a whim or a vice? (For not a few transvestites have committed suicide on account of their inability to "live their life".) Is it not rather something inborn, something which is stronger than themselves, stronger than their "will-power," stronger than their fear of disgrace and of punishment? A peculiarity—or call it abnormality if you wish—that is so powerful needs to be treated differently than by brutal prison sentences.

And whom does it harm if a man wears woman's clothes or vice versa? The disease is certainly not infectious. No normal man or woman will want to don the clothes of the other sex because some transvestites are permitted to parade in them.

However, this is not a treatise nor even an essay on Transvestitism, and this is not what I started out to write about. I have started out to write about Dr. Magnus Hirschfeld and his Institute of Sexual Science. Both are worth writing about, because both have done and are doing a great deal for our miserable, suffering, groping-in-the-dark humanity.

It is my fond belief that those who have been clearing away the debris which during two thousand years has accumulated in and befouled the field of sex will be counted, in time to come, among humanity's real benefactors. And among these benefactors, Dr. Magnus Hirschfeld, clear-sighted, non-sensational, humane, will occupy a most honored place. I have always been saying: The sex life of two normal adults is their own affair, and their own affair only; and it is the height of impudence, it is trampling upon the private life of individuals for the State to interfere and push in its paws. Dr. Hirschfeld has gone further, and he has proclaimed: The sex life of two individuals, normal or abnormal, is their own affair and their own affair only, and the State has no right to interfere in the matter. And by boldly proclaiming and proving that homosexuals, transvestites and other abnormals (I use the word abnormal: he refuses to use it, employing the word "variants" instead) are not degenerates, not vicious criminals, not even generally inferior to normal people, he has given back their self-respect and has made life bearable to thousands and thousands of unfortunates whose life had been a hell before. And he has saved thousands from a suicide's grave. And he has made the field very dangerous and unprofitable for the dastardly blackmailer, whose particular domain of activity is among the sexually abnormal, and who thrives with such peculiar luxuriance in our puritanical country.

The Institute of Sexual Science (Institut für Sexualwissenschaft) is an outgrowth and development of the Scientific-Humanitarian Committee whose purpose was—and still is—the protection of the homosexuals and the abolition of the German law against homosexuality.

The scope of the Institute is a much wider one, embracing as it does the entire field of sexology. It is an institution absolutely unique in the whole world. It is an institution of which I dreamed for many years and which I hoped to establish in the United States but which I felt would not thrive on account of our prudish, hypocritical attitude to all questions of sex. In such an institution one has to have a free hand: the advice given must be unhampered by any fear of violating some medieval law or of colliding with a stupidly childish, and for that reason all the more tyrannical public opinion. What can be done in barbarous Europe cannot always be done in ultra-civilized North America.

What is the scope of The Institute of Sexual Science? Instead of enumerating its various divisions, I will indicate the classes of cases that come there for counsel and treatment. For counsel, advice plays here as great a role as, nay, a greater role than treatment in its narrower sense.

1. A couple comes in to see the *Sanitätsrat*. They have decided to get divorced, they can not stand it any longer. *He* complains that she refuses to have any sexual relations whatever; has not permitted any for a year. *She* admits it, but claims that is because of his impotence; he never gave her any satisfaction; only left her in an irritated and nervous condition. Soothing explanations, certain advice, decide the couple to postpone their divorce and to try again for a time.

2. A poor woman wants contraceptive advice. She has five children already, and in these hard times she thinks it is enough. The doctors think so too, and she gets the advice; quite gratis. I might say here that sixty to seventy percent of all patients applying at the Institute are advised and treated free.

3. A man wants to find out if anything can be done for his wife who is insanely jealous without any reason and who threatens his and her own life. Evidently a dangerous psychosis, but he is told to bring her along the next day.

4. Man complains of Ejaculatio Praecox, and wants to know if the Steinach operation will do him good.

5. Another man. Suffering from lack of libido and impotence. Wants to get married. Is referred to the proper department.

6. A couple, a pretty, young couple, want to know if they are fit to get married—want a complete physical examination.

7–8. One patient with gonorrhea, one with lues. They are referred to the proper department.

9. A homosexual wants to have his beard destroyed by the X-ray so he won't have to shave, and be reminded of his male attribute. It is done.

10. A woman, non-homosexual, distressed over her beard-growth wants to have a complete epilation.

11. A number of homosexuals, for advice, etc.

12. Ditto transvestites.

13. A homosexual wants to have castration performed upon him. If it isn't done, he threatens to do it himself. He hates the thought, the very idea of the male genitals.

14. A pregnant woman, tubercular and nephritic, wants to have her pregnancy interrupted. She is examined and an affirmative answer is given to her request.

15. A woman has been married five years; has never been pregnant. Wants a child.

16. Woman suffering from vaginismus.

17. Man wants his semen examined for fertility.

18. Young couple want to know if it is safe for them to get married: they are first cousins.

19. Mother brings her daughter who is twenty years old and has never menstruated.

20. Young man wants a Wassermann made.

21. Mother brings her boy of fourteen who is masturbating excessively.

22. Another mother brings her young daughter suffering with schizophrenia.

23. An extremely peculiar case of shoe fetichism.

24. Man wants to know the normal frequency of coitus so as not to hurt himself nor his wife.

25. A case of adiposis genitalis.

I could go on giving dozens of other examples, but the above will suffice to show the scope of the Institute as far as patients are concerned: It is a Eugenic, Marriage Consultation and General Consultation bureau on all questions of normal and abnormal sexuality, and a diagnostic-therapeutic clinic of physical and psychic disorders (as well as venereal and skin diseases).

But it is much more than that. Physicians from various countries come to examine the numerous pictures, apparatus, albums, moulages and chamber of horrors dealing with various phases of human sexuality; people come to consult the sex library connected with the Institute; lawyers come to get points for the defense of their clients who happen to get caught in the clutches of the law (and Dr. Hirschfeld is in great demand as an expert in sex cases). And then there are lectures, lectures and lectures, on all subjects connected with sexology and sex reform. The Ernst Haeckel Hall, which forms a part of the Institute, is frequently packed with physicians and laymen, and the lectures delivered there have no doubt contributed much to shed light on many moot sex questions and have helped to foster a more liberal, more tolerant attitude towards all abnormals or as Dr. Hirschfeld calls them "variants."

One may visit and read about a country and still know very little about it. To know the heart of a country you must live in it. I had visited the Institute and read about it, but still it is only now, after having lived in it, that I appreciate fully its value and its importance. For his untiring, unselfish work, Dr. Hirschfeld will deserve a monument. Perhaps posterity will erect him one. But whether a monument is built him or not, the Institute, if it continues to live and uphold the ideals he has laid down in its foundation, will be *aere perennius*, a more permanent monument than one of bronze. It will certainly be a more useful one.

I should like to say something about the staff of the Institute, about their friendly co-operation, about their deep loyalty to their chief, their love and affection for him—but perhaps this would be touching too closely upon the personal.—I cannot however conclude without expressing a deep wish that such institutes might exist in every large city, or at least in every large capital. The United States could certainly use five or six such institutes—say one in New York, one in Boston, one in Chicago, one in Atlanta, one in San Francisco. They would all have plenty of work to do, and less ignorance and consequently less misery in sex matters would be the result.

When I get back to New York I may try to establish the first institute of this kind in the United States—thus doing on a large scale what I have been doing on a small scale for a quarter of a century.

And then again I may not: too much hard, nerve-wracking work.

I see that I have omitted one division of the work of the Institute, and that is consultations about choosing a profession or a trade, advice as to the handling of boys who have already had to do with juvenile courts, questions of the bringing up of "difficult," somewhat abnormal, psychopathic or neuropathic children, etc. This is an important department and its importance is bound to grow greater and greater as time goes on. Such consultation bureaus ought to exist not only in every large city; there ought to be something similar in every small town as well. Hoodlumism and juvenile criminality would be growing less instead of spreading more and more widely.

In conclusion, it may be of interest for my readers to know that the Institute is now not Dr. Hirschfeld's personal property. It was; but on February 2, 1924, he has made it over, with all its real estate, laboratories, apparatus, collections, archives, library, etc., to the State, and it is now State property. And the official name of it is The Institute of Sexual Science—The Dr. Magnus Hirschfeld Foundation. May the Foundation be built on a permanent, never to be shaken foundation.

(*Medical Critic and Guide*, vol. 25C, October 1925, pp 391–396.)

Appendix 2

IN HONOR OF MAGNUS HIRSCHFELD*
Victor Robinson

Among the ancient Egyptian papyri, there is one known as the Papyrus of Set, which is devoted largely to the subject of sexual anomalies. Like most things Egyptian, it is rather vague to our occidental understanding, and it is not until we reach the more familiar ground of Greece and Rome that we find copious material. Numerous deviations from normal sexuality are recorded in the narrative of Herodotus, father of history; and Hippocrates, father of medicine, gave to his contemporaries, and to posterity, a masterly description of sexual impotence. Among the Latin writers, we find inexhaustible sources in the biographies of Suetonius, the amatory poems of Ovid and Catullus, in the annals of Tacitus, the sham-smashing satires of Juvenal, and those terrible epigrams of Martial.

One would suppose that with a background extending to so distant an era, mankind would have achieved wisdom, but once again Clio teaches us that time alone does not bring wisdom to nations any more than to individuals—and in this field particularly, the passing centuries, under the influence of Judeo-Christian asceticism, went backward. The Dark Ages in medicine lasted only until the Renaissance, but the Dark Ages in sexology persisted until the dawn of the Twentieth Century.

For example, toward the end of the Nineteenth, in the most celebrated of all trials dealing with sexual anomalies, the mental processes of the magistrates were reminiscent of medieval inquisitors judging a heretic. Justice Wills murdered Oscar Wilde—more slowly, but as surely as Bishop Cyril murdered Hypatia. Ignorance and Intolerance sat on the woolsack at Old Bailey; little wonder the famous victim exclaimed, "How much more enlightened were the Greeks in these matters!" and said of himself, "I am a Greek born out of due time."

Sexology as a rational science belongs almost wholly to the Twentieth Century, and in this field there is no name more honorably conspicuous than that of Magnus Hirschfeld. The history of the modern phase of sexual science cannot be written without reference to his work on the erotic world-picture, the homosexual problem, the specificity of the sex hormones, castration in cases of moral crime, crises of puberty, heredity and the sex urge—work based on over thirty years of research and experience.

Dr. Hirschfeld, because of the great Institute of Sexual Science which you have established in Berlin; because of the important work you have there accomplished, and the impetus you have given to other workers; because you have shown there are no gaps in Nature, and that between the normal male and the normal female, there are all gradations of feminine males and masculine females; because you have dispelled long-untouched taboos with new knowledge; because where magistrates have written "voluntary viciousness," you have crossed out the words with "endocrine imbalance"; and because for many years you have been as a father to the stepchildren of nature— the American Society of Medical History, here assembled, considers it a privilege to welcome you as its honored guest.

---

*Welcoming Address at the reception in honor of Magnus Hirschfeld, under the auspices of the American Society of Medical History (December 4, 1930), on which occasion Dr. Hirschfeld addressed the Society on the History of Sexology. Since that time, on the day of the 'burning of the books,' his INSTITUT FUER SEXUALWISSENSCHAFT was wrecked, to the irreparable loss of sexual science. And amid the blazing torches and triumphant shouts of the Nazis, the head of Magnus Hirschfeld was carried in effigy. Hirschfeld now lives in exile. Such is Christian Civilization today.

(*Medical Review of Reviews*—Anthropos I 40 (458), pp. 49–51)

Bibliography

WORKS OF MAGNUS HIRSCHFELD IN ENGLISH

This compilation is based on information from an unpublished manuscript for the second edition of *The Writings of Magnus Hirschfeld* (2000) by James D. Steakley. Works found since then have been added.

1897

Hirschfeld, Magnus. "Petition to the Judiciary of the German Reich Regarding a Change of Paragraph 175 of the Reichsstrafgesetzbuch, and to the Reichstag Which Would Deal with It Afterward." In *Magnus Hirschfeld: Portrait of a Pioneer in Sexology* by Charlotte Wolff, 445–49. London: Quartet, 1986.

———."Petition to the Reichstag." In *We Are Everywhere: A Historical Soucebook of Lesbian and Gay Politics*, edited by Mark Blasius and Shane Phelan, 135–37. New York: Routledge, 1997.

1898

———."Questionnaire No. __." Translated by Margarete Nunberg. In *Minutes of the Vienna Psychoanalytic Society*, vol. 1: 1906–1908, edited by Herman Nunberg and Ernst Federn, 379–88. New York: International Universities Press, 1962.

———. *Research on Love between Men*. Translated by Michael A. Lombardi. Los Angeles: Urania Manuscripts, 1978.

1901

———. "The Social Problem of Sexual Inversion." Issued by the British Society for the Study of Sex Psychology. London: C. W. Beaumont. Reprinted in *A Homosexual Emancipation Miscellany, c. 1835–1952*, edited by Jonathan Ned Katz, 138–42. New York: Arno Press, 1975. Also reprinted in *We Are Everywhere: A Historical Sourcebook of Lesbian and Gay Politics*, edited by Mark Blasius and Shane Phelan. New York: Routledge, 1997.

1907

———. Epilogue to *Memoirs of a Man's Maiden Years* by N. O. Body, 109–11. Translated by Deborah Simon. Preface by Sander L. Gilman. Afterword by Hermann Simon. Philadelphia, PA: University of Pennsylvania Press, 2005.

1909

———. "Three Graves in a Distant Land." Translated by Michael Lombardi. Los Angeles: Urania Manuscripts, 1985. Reprinted in *Sodomites and Urnings: Homosexual Representations in Classic German Journals*, 41–46. Edited by Michael A. Lombardi-Nash. Binghamton: Harrington Park Press, 2006. Appeared simultaneously in *Journal of Homosexuality* 51/1 (2006).

1910

———. *Transvestites: The Erotic Drive to Cross-Dress*. Translated by Michael A. Lombardi-Nash. Introduction by Vern L. Bullough. Amherst, NY: Prometheus Books, 1991.

1911

———. "Theses for the Discussion of Sexual Abstinence." With Iwan Bloch. In *Sexual Continence and Its Influence on the Physical and Mental Health of Men and Women*, edited by William J. Robinson, 131–35. New York: Critic and Guide, 1924.

1912

———. Preface to *Die deutsche Wandervogelbewegung als erotisches Phänomen: Ein Beitrag zur Erkenntnis der sexuellen Inversion* (The German Wandervogel Movement as an Erotic Phenomenon: A Contribution Toward Understanding Sexual Inversion). By Hans Blüher. Translated by Richard Mills. *Gay Sunshine* (San Francisco) 42–43 (1980): 22.

1914

———. "Adaptation Treatment of Homosexuality (Adjustment Therapy)." Translated by Henry Gerber. *Homophile Studies* 5/2–4 (1962): 41–54.

———. "Adjustment Therapy." Translated by Richard Plant. In *Gay American History* by Jonathan Ned Katz, 151–53. New York: Thomas Y. Crowell, 1976. Reprinted New York: Avon, 1978, 231–35; New York: Harper & Row, 1985, 151–53; New York: Meridian, 1992.

———. "Classification of Homosexuals as to Age Preferences and Sex Acts." Translated by Henry Gerber. *Homophile Studies* 5/1 (1962): 20–29.

———. "Homosexuality in Philadelphia, Boston, Chicago, Denver, and New York." Translated by James Steakley. In *Gay American History* by Jonathan Ned Katz, 49–51. New York: Thomas Y. Crowell, 1976. Reprinted New York: Avon, 1978, 76–80; New York: Harper & Row, 1985, 49–51; New York: Meridian, 1992.

———. *The Homosexuality of Men and Women*. Translated by Michael A. Lombardi-Nash. Amherst, NY: Prometheus Books, 2000.

———. "The Role of Homosexual Men & Women in Society." Translated by Henry Gerber. *Homophile Studies* 6/1–2 (1963): 22–30.

1915

———. "Sexual Hypochrondria and Morbid Scrupulousness." In *Sexual Truths Versus Sexual Lies, Misconceptions and Exaggerations*. Edited by William J. Robinson. Hoboken: American Biological Society, 1919, 207–26. Reprinted in 1927, 1932, and 1937.

1917-20

———. *Sexual Pathology*. Abridged translation by Jerome Gibbs. Newark: Julian, 1932. Second edition, New York: Emerson, 1939; 3rd ed., 1940; 4th ed., 1945; 5th ed., 1947.

1923

———. "Introduction to Open Letter by Emma Goldman Concerning Louise Michel." Translated by James Steakley. In *Gay American History* by Jonathan Ned Katz, 377–78. New York: Thomas Y. Crowell, 1976. Reprinted New York: Avon, 1978; New York: Harper & Row, 1985; New York: Meridian, 1992.

1926

———. "Sexual Catastrophes." Translated by Don Reneau. In *The Weimar Republic Sourcebook*, edited by Anton Kaes, Martin Jay, and Edward Dimendberg, 700–701. Berkeley: University of California Press, 1994.

———. "Sexual Ipsation, Its Causes and Results." *Medical Critic and Guide* 25 (9 September 1926): 356–63.

1929

———. "The Development and Scope of Sexology." In *The Weimar Republic Sourcebook*, edited by Anton Kaes, Martin Jay, and Edward Dimendberg, 708–10. Berkeley: University of California Press, 1994.

1930

———. "The Conception of Indecency." In *World League for Sexual Reform. Proceedings of the Third Congress, London, 8–14 September 1929*, edited by Norman Haire, 637. London: Kegan Paul, Trench, Trubner.

———. "Letter to Dr. Harry Benjamin dated 1 March 1930." Translated and introduced by Erwin J. Haeberle. In *Bashers, Baiters & Bigots: Homophobia in American Society*, edited by John De Cecco, 132. New York and Binghamton: Harrington Park Press, 1984. Appeared simultaneously in *Journal of Homosexuality* 10/1–2.

———. "Love Awakening in America Observed by Dr. Hirschfeld in a Dialogue with George Sylvester Viereck," *Chicago Herald and Examiner*, November 30, 1930. Appeared simultaneously in other Hearst newspapers, including the *Albany Times-Union, Detroit Times, Los Angeles Examiner, New York American, Pittsburgh Sun-Telegraph, Rochester Sunday American, Washington Herald*.

———. "Marriage Bureaux." In *World League for Sexual Reform: Proceedings of the Third Congress, London, 8–14 September 1929*, edited by Norman Haire, 661. London: Kegan Paul, Trench, Trubner.

———. "Presidential Address." In *World League for Sexual Reform. Proceedings of the Third Congress, London, 8–14 September 1929*, edited by Norman

Haire, xi–xv. London: Kegan Paul, Trench, Trubner.

———. *The Sexual History of the World War*. In Collaboration with World-Famous Physicians, Scientists and Historians. New York: Panurge, 1934. Second edition, New York: Falstaff, 1937; 3rd ed., New York: Cadillac, 1941; 4th rev. ed., by Edward Podolsky, 1946.

———. "War Brothels." In *Morals in Wartime*, edited by Victor Robinson, 661. New York: Publishers Foundation, 1943.

1931

———. "Could You Answer These Questions When You Were Married? As Told to George Sylvester Viereck." *Liberty* 8/34 (1931): 18–22.

———. "'Dr. Einstein of Sex' Not So Favorably Impressed by U.S. in a Dialogue with George Sylvester Viereck." *Wisconsin News* (Milwaukee), February 2, 1931. Appeared simultaneously, in some instances with a different title, in other Hearst newspapers, including the *Albany Times-Union, Chicago Herald and Examiner, Detroit Times, Los Angeles Examiner, New York American, Pittsburgh Sun-Telegraph, San Francisco Examiner, Seattle Post-Intelligencer, Washington Herald.*

———. "Harlem's Emotional Beauty Charms 'Einstein of Sex' in a Dialgue with George Sylvester Viereck." *Wisconsin News* (Milwaukee), February 3, 1931. Appeared simultaneously in the *Chicago Herald and Examiner*.

———. "Hirschfeld Asks Scientific Sex View, Not Theological in a Dialgue with George Sylvester Viereck." *Wisconsin News* (Milwaukee), February 4, 1931. Appeared simultaneously in the *Chicago Herald and Examiner*.

———. "Sexual Reform on a Scientific Basis." *Earth*, March 1931.

———. "What Is This Thing Called Love?" *Physical Culture* 65/6 (1931): 56, 138–40.

1932

———. "Letter to the Editor." *Estia* (Athens), March 25, 1932. Reprinted in *Vradyne* (Athens), March 28, 1932. *Journal of Homosexuality* 34/1 (1932): 23–24. In *Magnus Hirschfeld in Greece* by Panayiotis Vyras, 1997.

1934

———. "Excerpt of Undated Letter to William J. Robinson." *Medical Critic and Guide* 32, (1934): 152–53. In *Sexologic Literature Pirates* by William J. Robinson.

1935

———. *Sex in Human Relationships*. Translated by John Rodker. With an introduction by Norman Haire. International Library of Sexology and Psychology. London: John Lane. Reprinted New York: AMS Press, 1975.

———. *Women East and West. Impressions of a Sex Expert.* London: William Heinemann.

1933-1937

———. "Hindu Sexology." In *The Hindu Art of Love*. Edited by Edward Windsor [S. Malkin], vi–viii. New York: Falstaff.

1936

———. "Hirschfeld, Magnus," signed autobiographical sketch. In *Encyclopaedia Sexualis: A Comprehensive Encyclopaedia-Dictionary of the Sexual Sciences*, edited by Victor Robinson, 317–21. New York: Dingwall-Rock. Reprinted in *A Homosexual Emancipation Miscellany, c. 1835–1952*, edited by Jonathan Ned Katz. New York: Arno, 1975.

———. "Homosexuality." In *Encyclopaedia Sexualis: A Comprehensive Encyclopaedia-Dictionary of the Sexual Sciences*, edited by Victor Robinson, 321–34. New York: Dingwall-Rock. Reprinted as "The Homosexual as an Intersex." In *The Homosexuals: As Seen by Themselves and Thirty Authorities*, edited by Aron M. Krich, 119–34. New York: Citadel, 1954.

———. *Sexual Anomalies and Perversions. Physical and Psychological Development and Treatment. A Summary of the Works of the Late Professor Dr. Magnus Hirschfeld. Compiled as a Humble Memorial by His Pupils. A Textbook for Students, Psychologists, Criminologists, Probation Officers, Judges and Educationists.* By Arthur Koestler and Norman Haire. London: Francis Aldor. Second ed. (1944); 3rd ed., London: Torch (1946). Issued under the title *Sexual Anomalies*, New York: Emerson, 1944; 2nd rev. ed., 1948. Issued under the title *Sexual Anomalies and Perversions*, edited by Norman Haire. London: Encyclopaedic Press, 1953; New York: Emerson, 1956. Photocopy, Ann Arbor: University Microfilms International, 1981.

1938

———. "Letter to Dr. Harry Benjamin Dated 3 June 1934." In *The Birth of Sexology: A Brief History in Documents* by Erwin J. Haeberle, 45. Privately printed.

———. *Racism*. London: Victor Gollancz/Left Book Club Edition.

HIRSCHFELD'S MAJOR WORKS AVAILABLE ONLY IN GERMAN

1896

Ramien, Th. [Magnus Hirschfeld]. *Sappho und Sokrates oder Wie erklärt sich die Liebe der Männer und Frauen zu Personen des eigenen Geschlechts?* (Sappho and Socrates, or What Explains the Love of Men and Women for Members of Their Own Sex?). Leipzig: Max Spohr.

1903

Hirschfeld, Magnus. "Ursachen und Wesen des Uranismus" (Causes and Nature of Uranianism). *Jahrbuch für sexuelle Zwischenstufen* (Yearbook for Sexual Intermediacy) 5:1–193. Reprinted in *Documents of the Homosexual Rights Movement in Germany, 1836–1927*, edited by James Steakley. New York: Arno Press, 1975.

1912

———. *Naturgesetze der Liebe. Eine gemeinverständliche Untersuchung über den Liebes-Eindruck, Liebes-Drang und Liebes-Ausdruck mit zwei erläuternden Tafeln in Farbendruck* (Natural Laws of Love. An Exoteric Investigation of the Impression of Love, the Impulse to Love and the Expression of Love with Two Explanatory Color Charts). Berlin: Pulvermacher.

1917–1920

———. *Sexualpathologie. Ein Lehrbuch für Ärzte und Studierende. Erster Teil: Geschlechtliche Entwicklungsstörungen. Zweiter Teil: Sexuelle Zwischenstufen. Das männliche Weib und der weibliche Mann. Dritter Teil: Störungen im Sexualstoffwechsel mit besonderer Berücksichtigung der Impotenz* (Sexual Pathology. A Textbook for Physicians and Students. Part One: Disorders of Sexual Development. Part Two: Sexual Intermediacy. The Masculine Woman and the Feminine Man. Part Three: Disorders of Sexual Metabolism with Particular Emphasis on Impotence). Bonn: Marcus & Weber.

1926–1930

———. *Geschlechtskunde. Fünf Bände. 1. Band: Die körperseelischen Grundlagen. 2. Band: Folgen und Folgerungen. 3. Band: Einblicke und Ausblicke. 4. Band: Bilderteil. 5. Band: Registerteil.* (Sexology. Five Volumes. Volume 1: Psychosomatic Fundamentals. Volume 2: Consequences and Inferences. Volume 3: Insights and Outlooks. Volume 4. Illustrations). Stuttgart: Püttmann.

1986

———. *Von einst bis jetzt. Geschichte einer homosexuellen Bewegung 1897–1922* (From Then Until Now. History of a Homosexual Movement 1897–1922). Edited by Manfred Herzer and James Steakley. Schriftenreihe der Magnus Hirschfeld Gesellschaft (Monograph Series of the Magnus Hirschfeld Society) 1. West Berlin: Rosa Winkel.

WORKS ABOUT HIRSCHFELD IN ENGLISH

Bauer, J. Edgar. "Magnus Hirschfeld: Panhumanism and the Sexual Cultures of Asia," *Intersections: Gender, History and Culture in the Asian Context* 14 (2006), http://intersections.anu.edu.au/issue14/bauer.html.

———. "Magnus Hirschfeld's Doctrine of Sexual Intermediaries and the Transgender Politics of (No-)Identity." In *Past and Present of Radical Sexual Politics*, edited by Gert Hekma. Amsterdam: Mosse Foundation for the Promotion of Gay and Lesbian Studies at the University of Amsterdam, 2004, 41–55, http://www2.hu-berlin.de/sexology/BIB/bauer02.htm.

Brennan, Toni, and Peter Hegarty. "Magnus Hirschfeld, His Biographies and the Possibilities and Boundaries of 'Biography' as 'Doing History.'" *History of the Human Sciences* 22/5 (2009): 24–46.

Dose, Ralf. "The World League for Sexual Reform: Some Possible Approaches." In *Sexual Cultures in Europe. National Histories*, edited by Franz X. Eder, Lesley Hall, and Gert Hekma, 242–59. Manchester: Manchester University Press, 1999. Also in *Journal of the History of Sexuality* 12/1 (2003): 1–15, http://muse.jhu.edu/login?auth=0&type=summary&url=/journals/journal_of_the_history_of_sexuality/v012/12.1dose.pdf.

———. *Thirty Years of Collecting Our History—Or How to Find Treasure Troves*. Magnus-Hirschfeld-Gesellschaft e.V. Berlin, 2012, http://www.hirschfeld.in-berlin.de/publikationen/dose_alms.pdf.

Fuechtner, Veronika. "Indians, Jews and Sex: Magnus Hirschfeld and Indian Sexology." In *Imagining Germany Imagining Asia: Essays in Asian-German Studies*, edited by Veronika Fuechtner and Mary Rhiel, 111–130. Studies in German Literature, Linguistics, and Culture. Rochester, NY: Camden House, 2013.

Herrn, Rainer. "On the History of Biological Theories of Homosexuality." In *Sex, Cells, and Same-Sex Desire: The Biology of Sexual Preference*, edited by John de Cecco und David Allen Parker, 31–56. New York, London, Norwood: Harrington Park Press, 1995. And in *Journal of Homosexuality*, 28.

———. *100 Years Gay Rights Movement in Germany*. Exhibition Catalogue. New York: Goethe Institute, 1997.

Ivory, Yvonne "The Urning and His Own: Individualism and the Fin-de-Siècle Invert." *German Studies Review* 26/2 (2003): 333–352.

Johansson, Warren [Joseph Wallfield]. "Hirschfeld, Magnus (1868–1935)." In *Encyclopedia of Homosexuality*, 536–39. New York, London: Garland, 1990.

———. "Hirschfeld, Magnus." In *Gay & Lesbian Literature*, edited by Sharon Malinowski, 182–84. Detroit, London: St. James Press, 1994.

Leser, Hedwig. "The Hirschfeld Institute for Sexual Science." In *The Encyclopedia of Sexual Behaviour*, edited by Albert Ellis and Albert Abarbanel, vol. 2, 967–70. New York: Hawthorn Books and London: Corsano Co., 1961.

Lewis, Brian. Review of *Magnus Hirschfeld and the Quest for Sexual Freedom: A History of the First International Sexual Freedom Movement*, by Elena Mancini. *Journal of the History of Sexuality* 22/2 (2013): 351–53.

Magnus-Hirschfeld-Gesellschaft (Magnus Hirschfeld Society) *Institut für Sexualwissenschaft (1919–1933)—The Institute for Sexual Science—Instituto de Sexología. Ausstellung—Exhibition—Exposición*. Magnus-Hirschfeld-Gesellschaft: Berlin, 2002, http://www.hirschfeld.in-berlin.de/institut/en/index.html and CD-ROM. Website reviewed by Hubert Kennedy in *Journal for the History of Sexuality* 12/1: 122–26.

McLeod, Don. *Serendipity and the Papers of Magnus Hirschfeld: The Case of Ernst Maass*. IHLIA ALMS: Amsterdam, 2012, http://lgbtialms2012. blogspot.nl/2012/07/serendipity-and-papers-of-magnus.html.

Mancini, Elena. *Magnus Hirschfeld and the Quest for Sexual Freedom: A History of the First International Sexual Freedom Movement*. New York: Palgrave Macmillan, 2010.

Newton, Alistair. "The Legacy of Magnus Hirschfeld. A Gay Liberation Movement Destroyed by Hatred." *Xtra!* 667 (2010): 17.

Illingworth Kerr Gallery. *PopSex!* Alberta College of Art and Design: Calgary, Alberta, 2011.

Robinson, Victor. "In Honor of Magnus Hirschfeld." *Medical Review of Reviews—Anthropos* 40/458 (1934): 49–51.

Robinson, William J. "The Institute of Sexual Science. The Only Institute of Its Kind in the World." *Medical Critic and Guide* (American) *Journal of Sexology and Humanity* 25 C (1925): 391–96.

———. "My 1930 TriSections VII—XIX." *Medical Critic and Guide (American) Journal of Sexology and Humanity* 28/8 (1930): 245–65.

———. "Nature's Sex Stepchildren." *Medical Critic and Guide (American) Journal of Sexology and Humanity* 25 C, no. 12 (1925): 475–77.

———. "Sexologic Literature Pirates." *Medical Critic and Guide (American) Journal of Sexology and Humanity* 32/6 (1934): 151.

———. "Sixty-Five Days in Europe," an excerpt of "A Nation in Distress." *Medical Critic and Guide (American) Journal of Sexology and Humanity* 23/11 (1920): 379–87.

Steakley, James D. "Cinema and Censorship in the Weimar Republic: The Case of *Anders als die Andern*." *Film History* 11/2 (1999): 181–203.

———. *The Homosexual Emancipation Movement in Germany*. New York: Arno Press, 1975. Fifth printing, Salem, NH: Ayer, 1992.

———. "Iconography of a Scandal: Political Cartoons and the Eulenburg Affair." *Visual Communication* 9/2 (1983): 20–51.

———. "Per Scientiam ad Justitiam: Magnus Hirschfeld and the Sexual Politics of Innate Homosexuality." In *Science and Homosexualities*, edited by Vernon A. Rosario, 133–54. New York: Routledge, 1997.

———. *The Writings of Dr. Magnus Hirschfeld: A Bibliography*. Schriftenreihe der Magnus-Hirschfeld-Gesellschaft (Monograph Series of the Magnus Hirschfeld Society) 2. Toronto: Canadian Gay Archives, 1985.

Viereck, George Sylvester. *Glimpses of the Great*. New York: Macaulay, 1930.

Wolff, Charlotte. *Magnus Hirschfeld: A Portrait of a Pioneer in Sexology*. London: Quartet Books, 1986.

ADDITIONAL REFERENCES

(MOSTLY IN GERMAN)

Bowers, Q. David, and Richard G. Doty. *A California Gold Rush History Featuring the Treasure from the* SS Central America: *A Source Book for the Gold Rush Historian and Numismatist.* Newport Beach, CA: California Gold Marketing Group, 2002.

Diebow, Hans. *Der ewige Jude* (The Eternal Jew). Munich: Eher, 1937.

Dobler, Jens, ed. *Prolegomena zu Magnus Hirschfelds Jahrbuch für sexuelle Zwischenstufen (1899–1923). Register—Editionsgeschichte—Inhaltsbeschreibungen.* (Prolegomena to Magnus Hirschfeld's Yearbook for Sexual Intermediacy (1899–1923). Index—Publishing History—Description of Contents). Schriftenreihe der Magnus Hirschfeld Gesellschaft (Monograph Series of the Magnus Hirschfeld Society) 11. Hamburg: von Bockel, 2004.

Dose, Ralf. "In memoriam Li Shiu Tong (1907–1993). Zu seinem 10. Todestag am 5.10.2003" (In memoriam Li Shiu Tong (1907–1993). On the 10th Anniversary of His Death, October 5, 2003). *Mitteilungen der Magnus-Hirschfeld-Gesellschaft* 35–36 (2003): 9–23.

———. *Magnus Hirschfeld. Deutscher—Jude—Weltbürger* (Magnus Hirschfeld. German—Jew—World Citizen). Germany: Hentrich & Hentrich, 2005.

———. "Zum Hirschfeld-Artikel in der *Encyclopedia of Homosexuality.*" (On Hirschfeld's Article in the *Encyclopedia of Homosexuality*). *Mitteilungen der Magnus-Hirschfeld-Gesellschaft* 15 (1991): 58–63.

———, ed. *Magnus Hirschfeld: Testament. Heft II* (Notebook II). Berlin: Hentrich & Hentrich, 2013.

———. "Einleitung, Nachwort" (Introduction, Afterword) in Kraß (2013), 7–8, 62–69.

Dose, Ralf, and Hans Günter Klein, eds. *Mitteilungen der Magnus Hirschfeld Gesellschaft.* (Bulletin of the Magnus Hirschfeld Society), 2nd revised and expanded edition. Vol. 1, nos. 1–9 (1983–1986); Vol. 2, Nos. 10–15 (1987–1991). Hamburg: von Bockel, 1992.

Ekkehard, E., ed. *Sigilla Veri. Ph. Stauff's Semi-Kürschner. Lexikon der Juden, -Genossen und -Gegner aller Zeiten und Zonen, insbesondere Deutschlands, der Lehren, Gebräuche, Kunstgriffe und Statistiken der Juden sowie ihrer Gaunersprache, Trugnamen, Geheimbünde, usw.* (Lexicon of the Jews, Their Associates and Opponents in All Ages and Regions, Especially Germany, of the Jews' Doctrines, Customs, Artifices and Statistics, as Well as Their Thieves' Argot, False Names, Secret Societies, etc.) Vol. 2: columns 1172–1210. Erfurt, Germany: Bodung, 1929.

Friedlaender, Benedict. "Die Liebe Platons im Lichte der modernen Biologie" (Plato's Love in the Light of Modern Biology). In *Gesammelte kleinere Schriften* (Collected Shorter Writings), 197–203. Berlin-Treptow: Bernhard Zack, 1909.

Gidlow, Elsa. *Elsa, I Come with My Songs: The Autobiography of Elsa Gidlow.* San Francisco: Druid Heights Press, 1986.

Hamer, Dean, and Peter Copeland. *The Science of Desire: The Search for the Gay Gene and the Biology of Behavior.* New York: Simon and Schuster, 1994.

Hekma, Gert, Harry Oosterhuis, and James Steakley, eds. *Gay Men and the Sexual History of the Political Left: Part I.* Binghamton: Haworth, 1995. Special Double Issue, *Journal of Homosexuality.*

Henry, George W. *Sex Variants: A Study of Homosexual Patterns.* New York and London: Hoeber, 1941.

Herrn, Rainer. *Schnittmuster des Geschlechts* (Sexual Patterns). Gießen: Psychosozial, 2008.

———. "Vom Traum zum Trauma. Das Institut für Sexualwissenschaft" (From Dream to Trauma: The Institute for Sexual Science). In *Magnus Hirschfeld. Ein Leben im Spannungsfeld von Wissenschaft, Politik und Gesellschaft* (Magnus Hirschfeld: Balancing Science, Politics and Society), edited by Elke-Vera Kotowski and Julius H. Schoeps, 173–99. Sifria Wissenschaftliche Bibliothek (Sifria Scienctific Library) 8. Berlin: be.bra wissenschaft, 2004.

Herzer, Manfred. *Magnus Hirschfeld. Leben und Werk eines jüdischen, schwulen und sozialistischen Sexologen* (Magnus Hirschfeld: Life and Work of a Jewish, Gay, Socialist Sexologist). Zweite, überarbeitete Auflage, 2nd rev. ed. Bibliothek rosa Winkel (Pink Triangle Library) 28; Schriftenreihe der Magnus Hirschfeld Gesellschaft (Monograph Series of the Magnus Hirschfeld Society) 10. Hamburg: MännerschwarmSkript, 2001.

———. Review of *Magnus Hirschfeld and the Quest for Sexual Freedom: A History of the First International Sexual Freedom Movement* by Elena Mancini. *Mitteilungen der Magnus-Hirschfeld-Gesellschaft* 46–47 (2011): 64–68.

Herzog, Dagmar. *Paradoxien der sexuellen Liberalisierung* (Paradoxes of Sexual Liberation). Hirschfeld-Lectures 1. Göttingen: Wallstein, 2013.

———. *Sex after Fascism: Memory and Morality in Twentieth-Century Germany.* Princeton: Princeton University Press, 2005.

Hiller, Kurt: das buch mit dem zitat über die abneigungen

Hirschfeld, Emanuel H. *The Heart and Blood-Vessels: Their Care and Cure and the General Management of the Body.* New York and London: Funk & Wagnalls, 1913, 4th ed., 1916.

Hirschfeld, Magnus. "Franziska Manns Lebenseintritt" (Franziska Mann's Entry into Life). In *Franziska Mann. Der Dichterin—Dem Menschen! zum 9. Juni 1919* (Franziska Mann. To the Poetess and the Person! June 9, 1919), 14ff. Jena: Landhausverlag, 1919.

———. "Literarisches Selbstbekenntnis. Zu meinem 60. Geburtstag" (My Literary Confession. On My 60th Birthday). *Die literarische Welt* 4/21–22 (1928): 11.

———. "Phantom Rasse, 11. Fortsetzung " (The Phantom of Race, eleventh installment). *Die Wahrheit* (Prague) 14/5 (1935).

LeVay, Simon. *Gay, Straight, and the Reason Why: The Science of Sexual Orientation.* Oxford: Oxford University Press, 2011.

Keilson-Lauritz, Marita. Review of *Durch Wissenschaft zur Gerechtigkeit? Textsammlung zur kritischen Rezeption des Schaffens von Magnus Hirschfeld,* edited by Andreas Seeck. *Zeitschrift für Sexualforschung* 17/4 (2004): 372–75.

Kesten, Hermann. *Dichter im Café* (Poets' Café). Munich: Knaur, 1959.

Kinder, Gary. *Ship of Gold in the Deep Blue Sea.* New York: Random House, 1998.

Kotowski, Elke Vera, and Julius H. Schoeps, eds. *Magnus Hirschfeld. Ein Leben im Spannungsfeld von Wissenschaft, Politik und Gesellschaft* (Magnus Hirschfeld: Balancing Science, Politics and Society). Sifria Wissenschaftliche Bibliothek (Sifria Scientific Library) 8. Berlin: be.bra wissenschaft, 2004.

Kraß, Andreas. *"Meine erste Geliebte": Magnus Hirschfeld und sein Verhältnis zur schönen Literatur* ("My First Love": Magnus Hirschfeld and Creative Literature). Hirschfeld-Lectures 2. Göttingen: Wallstein, 2013.

Kühl, Richard "... Aber in unserem Buch, Herr Sanitätsrat!" Fragen an Magnus Hirschfelds Publikationspraxis 1929–30" (". . . But in our book, Herr Medical Counselor!" Questions Regarding Magnus Hirschfeld's Publishing Practices 1929–30). *Mitteilungen der Magnus-Hirschfeld-Gesellschaft* 41–42 (2009): 32–42.

Lehmstedt, Mark. *Bücher für das dritte Geschlecht. Der Max Spohr Verlag in Leipzig. Verlagsgeschichte und Bibliographie (1881–1941)* (Books for the Third Sex. The Leipzig Publisher Max Spohr. A History of the Publishing House with Bibliography, 1881–1941). Wiesbaden: Harrassowitz i. Komm, 2002.

Lenz, Ludwig Levy. *Discretion and Indiscretion.* Cairo: al-Maaref Press, 1949.

Levy-Lenz, Ludwig. *Erinnerungen eines Sexual-Arztes. Aus den Memoiren eines Sexologen.* 5th ed. Baden-Baden: Wadi-Verlagsbuchhandlung, 1954.

Magnus-Hirschfeld-Gesellschaft (Magnus Hirschfeld Society), eds. *Magnus Hirschfeld: Leben und Werk. Ausstellungskatalog aus Anlass seines 50. Todestags, veranstaltet von der Magnus Hirschfeld Gesellschaft 1985* (Magnus Hirschfeld: His Life and Works. Exhibition Catalogue on the Occasion of the Fiftieth Anniversary of His Death, presented by the Magnus Hirschfeld Society, 1985). With an afterword to the second edition by Ralf Dose. Schriftenreihe der Magnus Hirschfeld Gesellschaft (Monograph Series of the Magnus Hirschfeld Society) 6. Hamburg: von Bockel, 1992.

Moll, Albert. "Paragraph 175" (Paragraph 175). *Die Zukunft* 51 (1905): 315–20.

———. "Zur Klärung des homosexuellen Problems, II" (Clarifying the Homosexual Problems, II). *Europa* 1 (1905): 1099–1101.

Mühsam, Erich. *Die Homosexualität* (Homosexuality). Munich: Belleville, 1996.

Schoeps, Hans Joachim. *Der homosexuelle Nächste* (The Homosexual Next-Door). Hamburg: Furche, 1963. Originally published in 1903.

Seeck, Andreas. *Durch Wissenschaft zur Gerechtigkeit? Textsammlung zur kritischen Rezeption des Schaffens von Magnus Hirschfeld* (Through Science to Justice? Collected Writings on the Critical Reception of Magnus Hirschfeld's Achievements). Geschlecht—Sexualität— Gesellschaft. Berliner Schriften zur Sexualwissenschaft und Sexualpolitik (Gender—Sexuality—Society. Berlin Publications on Sexology and Sexual Policy) 4. Münster: Lit, 2003.

Seidel, Ralf. "Sexologie als positive Wissenschaft und sozialer Anspruch. Zur Sexualmorphologie von Magnus Hirschfeld" (Sexology as Positive Science and Social Agenda. On the Sexual Morphology of Magnus Hirschfeld). Ph.D. diss., Munich, 1969.

Steakley, James D. *Die Freunde des Kaisers. Die Eulenburg-Affäre im Spiegel zeitgenössischer Karikaturen* (The Emperor's Friends. The Eulenburg Affair as Reflected in Contemporary Caricatures). Bibliothek rosa Winkel (Pink Triangle Library) 37. Hamburg: MännerschwarmSkript, 2004.

Thoma, Ludwig. *Sämtliche Beiträge aus dem Miesbacher Anzeiger: 1920/21* (Complete Publications in the Miesbach Gazette). Critical edition with commentary by Wilhelm Volkert. Munich and Zurich: Piper, 1989.

Volk und Rasse. Ausstellung des Deutschen Hygiene-Museums Dresden (Nation and Race. Exhibit of the German Museum of Hygiene, Dresden). Dresden: Deutscher Verlag für Volkswohlfahrt (German Publisher for National Welfare), 1934.

Witte, Emil. *Drei Siegfriedsrufe. An alle Verantwortlichen in deutschen Landen. Erster Siegfrieds-Ruf: An die Väter, Mütter & Lehrer deutscher Jungen* (Three Calls of Siegfried. To All Responsible Parties in German Territories. First Call of Siegfried: To the Fathers, Mothers & Teachers of German Boys). Berlin-Friedenau: privately published, 1914.

Notes

1. Marita. Keilson-Lauritz, review of *Durch Wissenschaft zur Gerechtigkeit? Textsammlung zur kritischen Rezeption des Schaffens von Magnus Hirschfeld*, ed. Andreas Seeck, *Zeitschrift für Sexualforschung* 17/4 (2004): 375.

2. Magnus Hirschfeld, *Mein Testament: Heft II*, edited and annotated by Ralf Dose (Berlin: Hentrich & Hentrich, 2013), 140. (Henceforth *Testament* II). *Testament II*, 57.

3. Harry Benjamin to Magnus Hirschfeld, September 20, 1933; copy from Kinsey Institute kept in the Archive of the Magnus Hirschfeld Society.

4. *Psychosomatic Medicine* 6/4 (1945): 253–54.

5. Alfred Kinsey had an early work of Hirschfeld's translated for him by Hedwig Leser, a German immigrant: *Magnus Hirschfeld: Das Ergebnis der statistischen Untersuchungen über den Prozentsatz der Homosexuellen* (Results of the Statistical Survey on the Percentage of Homosexuals) (Leipzig: Spohr, 1904). The translation exists as part of the so-called Hirschfeld Scrapbook at the Kinsey Institute for Research in Sex, Gender, and Reproduction in Bloomington, Indiana.

6. See Herzog, 2013 (German) and Herzog, 2005 (English).

7. Please see the works of J. Edgar Bauer referred to in n. 45.

8. See, for example, Moll, 1905a, 1905b.

9. See Friedländer, 1909.

10. Hermann Simon has determined the author's identity as Karl M. Baer. *Memoirs of a Man's Maiden Years*, 2006.

11. For a critical perspective, see Herzer, *Capri*; Lewis in *JHS*, 2013.

12. Hans Diebow, *Der ewige Jude,* Munich, 1937.

13. Hans Joachim Schoeps, *Der homosexuelle Nächste*, Hamburg, 1963, 86.

14. Ludwig Levy-Lenz. *Erinnerungen eines Sexual-Arztes. Aus den Memoiren eines Sexologen*, 5th ed. (Baden-Baden: Wadi-Verlagsbuchhandlung, 1954), 431.

15. *Testament II*, 57.

16. See untitled poem in *Fest-Zeitung zur silbernen Hochzeit von Friederik Hirschfeld mit Sanitaäthsrath Dr. Hermann Hirschfeld am 31. Mai 1880*

(Commemorative Newspaper on the Occasion of the Silver Wedding Anniversary of Friederike Hirschfeld and Medical Councilor Dr. Hermann Hirschfeld on May 31, 1880), 3.

17. Magnus Hirschfeld, "Literarisches Selbstbekenntnis. Zu meinem 60. Geburtstag" (Literary Self-Affirmation. On My 60th Birthday), *Die literarische Welt* 4/21–22 (1928): 11.

18. Magnus Hirschfeld, *Ursachen und Wesen des Uranismus* (Causes and Nature of Uranianism). *Jahrbuch für sexuelle Zwischenstufen* 5 (1903): 3–4. Reprinted in *Documents of the Homosexual Rights Movement in Germany, 1836–1927*, ed. James Steakley (New York: Arno Press, 1975).

19. Ludwig Levy-Lenz, *Discretion and Indiscretion* (Cairo: al-Maaref Press, 1949), 421–22.

20. *Von einst bis jetzt. Geschichte einer homosexuellen Bewegung 1897*–1922 (From Then until Now: The History of a Homosexual Movement 1897–1922), ed. and with an afterword by Manfred Herzer and James Steakley (Berlin: rosa Winkel, 1986).

21. Letter from Karl Giese to Max Hodann, August 2, 1935. Arbetarrörelsens Arkiv (Labor Movement Archive), Stockholm, Max Hodann samling, vol. 15. Copy in the archives of the Magnus Hirschfeld Society.

22. Original in the Schweizerisches Sozialarchiv (Swiss Social Archive), Zurich. Bestand Brupbacher, Ar 101. Copy in the archives of the Magnus Hirschfeld Society.

23. Magnus Hirschfeld, "Phantom Rasse," 11th installment in *Die Wahrheit* (Prague) 14/5 (1935): 8.

24. *Women East and West. Impressions of a Sex Expert* (London: William Heinemann, 1935), 297.

25. Ibid., 275.

26. Ibid., 271ff.

27. Emil Witte, *Drei Siegfriedsrufe. An alle Verantwortlichen in deutschen Landen. Erster Siegfrieds-Ruf: An die Väter, Mütter & Lehrer deutscher Jungen. Berlin-Friedenau: Selbstverlag 1914* (Three Calls of Siegfried. To all Responsible People in German Lands. First Call of Siegfried: To the Fathers, Mothers and Teachers of German Boys) (Berlin-Friedenau: self-published, 1914).

28. SigillaVeri (Ph. Stauff's Semi-Kürschner), *Lexikon der Juden, -Genossen und -Gegner aller Zeiten und Zonen, insbesondere Deutschlands, der Lehren, Gebräuche, Kunstgriffe und Statistiken der Juden sowie ihrer Gaunersprache, Trugnamen, Geheimbünde, usw* (Lexicon of the Jews, Their Associates and Opponents in All Ages and Regions, especially Germany, of the Jews' Doctrines, Customs, Artifices and Statistics, as Well as Their Thieves' Argot, False Names, Secret Societies, etc.), ed. E. Ekkehard, bol. 2 (Erfurt: Bodung, 1929), columns 1172–1210.

29. Ludwig Thoma, *Sämtliche Beiträge aus dem Miesbacher Anzeiger: 1920–21* (Complete Publications in the *Miesbach Gazette*). Critical edition with commentary by Wilhelm Volkert (München/Zürich: Piper, 1989).

30. *Der Eigene* 4, October 1925.

31. *Volk und Rasse: Ausstellung des Deutschen Hygiene-Museums Dresden* (Nation and Race: Exhibit of the German Museum of Hygiene, Dresden) (Dresden: Deutscher Verlag für Volkswohlfahrt, 1934), Abb. 10, S. 19: Vier Portraits "Jüdischer Typen," darunter ein Bild Hirschfelds (Four portraits of "Jewish Types," including an image of Hirschfeld), illus. 10, 19.

32. Berlin State Library of the Prussian Cultural Heritage Foundation, Manuscript Department, Blüher Estate, K 14; cited in Herzer, 55.

33. *Testament II*, 77ff. The original handwritten notebook does not have page numbers.

34. Ibid., 64.

35. J. Edgar Bauer, "Magnus Hirschfeld's 'Doctrine of Sexual Intermediacy' and the 'Theory of Sexual Intermediacy' of His Interpreters: Notes on Confusion in Reception History,"*Capri. Journal for Gay History*, May 2004, 44; with reference to Edgar J. Bauer, see "The Death of Adam. Historical-Philosophical Theses on Sexual Emancipation in the Works of Magnus Hirschfeld (1998)," in Andreas Seeck, ed., *Through Science toward Justice?* (Münster: Lit Verlag 2003), 133–55: and the debate with Manfred Herzer about this essay in the *Communications of the Magnus Hirschfeld Society.*

36. *Dichter im Café* (Munich, 1959), 418.

37. *Geschlechtskunde (Sexology)*, vol. 1, x.

38. Petition to the Reichstag (1897), in *We Are Everywhere: A Historical Sourcebook of Gay and Lesbian Politics*, ed. Mark Blasius and Shane Phelan (New York, London: Routledge, 1997), 135–37.

39. Second edition of 1902 reprinted in *Documents of the Homosexual Rights Movement in Germany, 1836–1927*, ed. James Steakley (New York: Arno, 1975). Issued in English as "The Social Problem of Sexual Inversion" (1903) by the British Society for the Study of Sex Psychology. Reprinted in *A Homosexual Emancipation Miscellany, c. 1835–1952*, ed. Jonathan Ned Katz (New York: Arno, 1975); and in Blasius and Phelan, *We Are Everywhere: A Historical Sourcebook of Lesbian and Gay Politics*, 138–42.

40. All quotations from Benedikt Friedlaender, *Die Liebe Platons im Lichte der modernen Biologie. Gesammelte kleinere Schriften* (Plato's Love in Light of Modern Biology) (Berlin, 1909), 197–230.

41. "Open Letter" (1904), in Erich Mühsam, *Die Homosexualität* (Homosexuality) (Munich, 1996), 75.

42. Dorchen was repeatedly examined at the institute and submitted to an early sex-change operation, with castration, amputation of the penis, and neo-vagina. Since she could not afford to pay the expense of her operations, she worked in the household of the institute. The figure "Dorchen" in Rosa von Praunheim's film *The Einstein of Sex* is complete fiction. See Rainier Herrn, *Schnittmuster des Geschlechts* (Patterns of Gender) (Giessen: Psychosozial-Verlag, 2004), p.201 et seq.

43. *Testament II*, 38.

44. Ibid.,49.

45. Ibid., 50.
46. Ibid., 47.
47. Ibid., 57.
48. Ibid., 60.
49. Ibid., 61.
50. *Women East and West,* xix.
51. *Testament II,* 62.
52. Magnus Hirschfeld, *Testament Heft II*, edited by Ralf Dose (Berlin: Hentrich & Hentrich, 2013), 79.
53. Ibid., 81.
54. Ibid., 90.
55. Ibid., 78.
56. Magnus Hirschfeld, *The Homosexuality of Men and Women*, trans. Michael Lombardi-Nash (Amherst, NY: Prometheus Books, 2000).
57. *Geschlechtskunde,* vol. 3, 8.
58. This story had been related elsewhere. See Ralf Dose, "In memoriam Li Shiu Tong (1907–1993). Zu seinem 10. Todestag am 5.10.2003" (In memoriam Li Shiu Tong. On the 10th anniversary of his death, October 5, 2003), in *Mitteilungen der Magnus-Hirschfeld-Gesellschaft* 35/36 (2003): 9–23.
59. Kinder, 2002.
60. Hirschfeld, 1919, 14ff.
61. *Testament II*.
62. *New York Times*, December 22, 1930. This appears to have been a special program compiled for screening especially at the Embassy Theater. Fox Movietone's "turnover sheets," which are still preserved, state that the Hirschfeld interview was sent to the archive by the editorial staff on December 5, 1930, which means it must have been filmed in the week of December 1–5, 1930. The "continuity sheets" from the newsreels distributed in December 1930 have also been preserved, but they contain no mention of the Hirschfeld interview. My thanks to Greg Wilsbacher, Moving Image Research Collections, University of South Carolina, for this information.
63. See Herrn, 2008.
64. William J. Robinson (1925), "The Institute of Sexual Science: The Only Institute of Its Kind in the World," in W. Robinson, ed., *Medical Critic and Guide. (American) Journal of Sexology and Humanity.* New York, 1925, 25 C, pp. 391–396.
65. This letter is kept at the Stadt- und Landesbibliothek Dortmund, Handschriftenabteilung (Manuscript Department of the Dortmund Municipal and Regional Library), Magnus Hirschfeld, Signature: Agt. 18717. It has been reproduced in full in *Testament II*, 223.
66. Henry, 1941.
67. Gidlow, 1986, 226ff.
68. *Testament II*, 108.
69. Ibid., 168.

Index